Hang on to Matthew 6:33

In sharing his life's journey of servanthood, Dr. King has rendered a great service to the church. The book is filled with wonderful, and at times poignant, stories of his own life and growth, as well as of warm family experiences. It's a "must read" autobiography.

> Dr. Florence Montz
> President Association of Lutheran Older Adults
> Valparaiso University

After reading Robert King's biography it is easy to see why his wife, Jean, said to him, "You pursue the work of two strong men and wonder why you feel on the run." Dr. King's extraordinary life story is a chronicle of perseverance and grace. Perseverance in that as an African American he had to overcome many obstacles—and as a man of faith, his story is a testimony to the power and love of God in the life of a human being. I strongly recommend this autobiography for anyone who'd want to know what it was like for a natural-born leader to grow up in a racially segregated society. The lessons are appropriate for us all!

> Rev. Dr. Robert Scudieri
> Area Secretary for North America World Missions
> The Lutheran Church–Missouri Synod

This book is a good example of an old African American expression, "God can make a way out of no way." Several times in pivotal periods in the life of this great man we see God doing just that. Must reading for those, who at times, doubt God's ability to make a way out of no way.

> Rev. Dr. William Griffin
> Employed staff
> Northern Illinois District, LCMS

Pastor Jenkins Said

"Hang on to Matthew 6:33"

Autobiography of
Robert H. King, Ph.D.

CPH.
Concordia Publishing House

For my wife, Jean; our children, Jocelyn, Jann, and Roger; and our grandson, Casey.

Copyright © 1999 Concordia Publishing House
3558 S. Jefferson Avenue, St. Louis, MO 63118-3968
Manufactured in the United States of America

3 4 5 6 7 8 9 10 11 12   10 09 08 07 06 05 04 03 02 01

Contents

Acknowledgments

Heartfelt words cannot adequately express the depth of my gratitude to those who helped immeasurably in the preparation of this autobiography. I owe many thanks to Jean, my faithful wife of 48 years, for her tireless efforts, insightful abilities, and literary experience in assisting with the editing of this life-reviewing material. I am especially grateful for the "Now, Jean" chapter I invited her to write in which she summarizes some of her memories.

Mrs. Mattie Chambers, next-door neighbor and faculty member at Jefferson City High School, is exceedingly praiseworthy for her professional secretarial work in preparing this book. Her patience was equal to her excellence in bringing this task to its final stage. Her understanding, cooperation, and skill were superb.

I wish to express sincere gratitude to Dr. August Suelflow, retired director of Concordia Historical Institute. He gave unrelenting motivation and invigorating encouragement in completing this life-story endeavor. This man of God appears to hold a vision of the value my story may have for young men and young women towards helping to shape lives in the Lord's kingdom work during the 21st century.

My final acknowledgment is this: "Hitherto hath the LORD helped us." (1 Samuel 7:12)

Preface

The book's title demonstrates Rev. R. F. Jenkins' profound influence on my life. Introductory information that follows is intended to lend some enlightenment and credence to a role model and mentor.

My first time meeting Rockefeller Jenkins was during the Alabama Pastors and Teachers Conference. I was 11 years old, singing with the Good Shepherd Lutheran School choir at the conference. He was a friendly young man, handsome, approximately six feet tall.

At first he seemed to have been one of the teachers. Jenkins would never have imagined the gratification I had meeting a young minister, my aspiration! In reality or through imagination, Jenkins appeared to be a very welcome and distinguished individual among the pastors and teachers at the conference.

Rockefeller's sister, Julia Jenkins, was my fifth- and sixth-grade teacher at Good Shepherd. Later, while attending Alabama Lutheran Academy, Selma, Mrs. Lou Jenkins, his mother was the matron. She was a devoted friend to the students without sacrificing her supervisory respect. We could discuss problems with her and receive wise counsel. I perceived her aura as equating a mother image for us.

Boys who attended school with R. F. Jenkins at Alabama Lutheran Academy referred to him as "Rock." They boasted about his outstanding ball playing, specifically as a home-run hitter.

During my years at the academy, I frequently heard pastors and teachers discuss Pastor Jenkins' articulate, eloquent speaking skills as he preached excellent sermons. Summarily, he was known as an effective pastor and teacher among Lutherans throughout Alabama.

Carrie Harper and I were the graduation class of 1937 at Good Shepherd Lutheran School. The Reverend R. F. Jenkins, our speaker, used the text Matthew 6:33, "Seek ye first the kingdom of God, and His righteousness; and all these things shall be added unto you." He exhorted us that our ultimate goal was to have God foremost in our lives. God's kingdom of grace and the hope of His glory were to be our paramount guideposts for persistent seeking and godly living. We were to firstly and continuously reach out for His righteousness by grace through faith in the redemptive sacrifice of Jesus Christ. In God's care, we experience His fulfillment and accomplishments for our lives as we ponder and pursue various desires and goals. Without seeking God's kingdom and righteousness, our efforts for life's fulfillment would be fruitless. We were admonished that there is no need to worry and to be greatly concerned about the anxieties, desires, and cares of life's situations. God's earthly blessings will come into being according to His good and gracious will. Pastor Jenkins' emphasis was in perfect accord with "but my God shall supply all your need according to His riches in glory by Christ Jesus" (Philippians 4:19).

While talking with him following graduation, and declaring my vigorous desire to go to high school facing the apparent nil probability of funds for tuition, he directed me to invest in Matthew 6:33 as I continued my pursuit. The book cites our encounter. Within this framework, a story of my life unobtrusively derives a title, and a tribute to Pastor Jenkins is signaled.

Recalling my earliest memories and during all my life's

journeying, parents and family members provided inspirational encouragement. Also, I have been heartened by clergy mentors and/or role models, among whom I must give specific reference to Pastors Albert Dominick, Henry Grigsby, Peter Hunt, Joseph Lavalais, R. O. L. Lynn, and J. T. Skinner. The Reverend Rockefeller Jenkins is in a distinctive focus because during a moment when I perceived a critical edge, he had a stirring call-to-faith-and-action talk with me.

Reflecting on occurrences in my life, especially those selected for this book, I am compelled to conclude, "If God be for us, who can be against us? He that spared not His own Son, but delivered Him up for us all, how shall He not with Him also freely give us all things?" (Romans 8:31–32).

(The decision to write my life story in the present tense was inspired by Bernard Selling, Ph.D., a college writing professor. Helpful information was studied in his *Writing from Within: A Unique Guide to Writing Your Life's Stories* [Hunter House, Inc.], 1990, 2nd ed.)

Foreword

BY REV. R. F. JENKINS

God's world contains countless problems. Some are small, some are large, and we might even think of middle sizes. With respect to all of them, God's admonition is, "Don't worry." Our lives would be quite different if we did not face problems; they can make or break us.

The writer of this book, Dr. Robert King, faced more problems than an ordinary person. Some of us can look into the past and see the mountains of troubles, the hills of hardships, the valleys of depression, and the streams of sorrow that he and some of us had to face. In spite of all of them, he has victoriously reached a plateau in life that makes me very proud. He did not achieve this alone or even by his power. God's strong hand and loving heart pulled him through and allowed him a life span of 49 years to serve Him in the ministry. I am grateful that God led him, so that he might lead others.

During the '30s, '40s, and '50s there were many Lutheran churches with parochial schools in Alabama. Pastors were asked to serve dual parishes and sometimes to teach school. After eight years in the ministry, I had one school to teach and five congregations to serve. One of these churches was just a few miles across the Alabama River from Good Shepherd School. In 1937 they invited me to give the graduation address. Robert King was one of the graduates.

The basis of my address was Matthew 6:33, "Seek ye first the kingdom of God, and His righteousness; and all these things shall be added unto you." I had no idea that these words were so meaningful to him. But now at the age of 85, I know that the Holy Spirit calls by the Gospel and accomplishes whatsoever He wills. May this book be a blessing to many people, and may God's matchless grace, boundless mercy, and endless love be showered upon him and his family.

Your friend in Christ,
R. F. Jenkins

Foreword

BY DR. AUGUST R. SUELFLOW

Here is the story of a king telling a story of our Lord's saints. The story conveys such a fascinating and interesting account that when you read it, you are not able to lay it down until you have finished it. It covers a period of our country and Lutheranism in America that remains unknown to many of our readers today. It is a story that should have the widest readership. It takes you into the south of our country at the time of the great financial depression and is filled with pathos, feeling, and emotion.

It is a most intriguing story with its ups and downs of life, moving from great health to severe sicknesses. The title itself is unique and intriguing and demonstrates the firm commitment of Dr. Robert H. King and his family coupled with the Lord's promises and help.

It is the account of a great African American pastor and church leader with his life's experiences of highs and lows, his life of service to God's people in the church, his remarkable innocence of racial differences. The book must be read by all at this turn of the millennium to reflect and to review what the first half of this century produced in our country, much to our shame. It is far from being a history lesson, but it is much more the confession of one man's faith and life together with his dear wife and family.

It is the type of story that the reader will enjoy, page after page while he is learning to follow our Lord Jesus Christ and His saints by walking and talking with them under various circumstances. It is full of human struggle and serious illness but always proclaiming God's perseverance and help. The account touches on human emotions and life situations common to us all.

A most interesting chapter deals with Dr. Marmaduke Carter, an African American patriarch in The Lutheran Church—Missouri Synod, who played a giant role in introducing African Americans to the descendants of German Lutherans in America. Dr. Carter's contributions are unequaled. (For example, the writer of this Foreword remembers hearing Dr. Carter preach at an outdoor mission festival in flawless German. It was an unusual experience, because at a similar festival Sunday he had also heard Sam Millev, a Native American chief who donned his war bonnet and Indian garb as he addressed the people. What a marvelous way to teach ethnicity and harmony among Christians.)

Dr. Carter was an extremely effective speaker, also in German, so that the hearers immediately forgot the color of his skin and remembered only his witness to Christ. Those who heard him never realized that there were barriers that had to be overcome.

The story is told of him that he traveled by train from Chicago to some northern Wisconsin community where he was to preach on Sunday morning. As Dr. Carter got off the train on Saturday evening, some railroad hands were preparing the train to move on to its next destination. One of them, in "Low" German, asked the other: "I wonder what that black man is doing in our town on Saturday night?" Still with his valise in hand, Dr. Carter responded to them in perfect Low German: "I will be preaching at your church tomorrow morning, and you boys better come to the service!"

Dr. Robert King, as Dr. Carter's vicar and successor in the parish, "inherited" a lot from his predecessor in the pastoral office and tells us about it.

Dr. and Mrs. King are both the holders of their personal Ph.D. degrees and have devoted a large part of their life to teaching in secondary and higher education, including Concordia Teachers College, River Forest, Ill., and more recently at Lincoln University, Jefferson City, Mo., as well as Concordia Seminary, St. Louis. Besides having the distinction of being the only African American pastor to serve a totally white congregation in the LCMS, Dr. King has been a vice-president of The Lutheran Church—Missouri Synod from 1986 to the present. Since 1989 he has been the elected second vice-president holding the third highest office in The Lutheran Church—Missouri Synod.

He and his dear wife, Jean, as well as the children have consistently remembered and experienced the encouraging words of Pastor Jenkins: "Seek ye first the kingdom of God, and His righteousness; and all these things shall be added unto you."

May each of the readers of this autobiography be cheered and lifted up to the cross of our Lord Jesus Christ.

Aug. R. Suelflow
Lent 1998

CHRONOLOGY

April 1, 1922   Born, Sunny South, Ala., eighth child of 16 children.

1925   Moved to Mingham, La. (spring).

Returned to Sunny South, Ala. (fall).

1928   Entered Kemp Grove School, Kemp Grove, Ala.

1929   Entered Thomasville Elementary School, Thomasville, Ala.

1930   No school available.

1931   Baptized in Cub Creek, sponsored by Shady Grove Baptist Church, Sunny South, Ala.

1932   Entered Good Shepherd Lutheran School, Vineland, Ala.

1934   Mother passed—leaving husband and nine children.

1937   Graduated from Good Shepherd Lutheran School, Vineland, Ala.

Matriculated at Alabama Lutheran Academy, Selma, Ala.

1938   Transferred to Westfield High School, Westfield, Ala.

1939   Reentered Alabama Lutheran Academy.

1941   Graduated from Alabama Lutheran Academy.

1941   Vacancy teacher at Bethlehem Lutheran School, Holy Ark, Ala.

1942   Employed at Maritime Shipyard, Mobile, Ala.

Drafted into the United States Army, Mobile, Ala.

1943   Received honorable discharge from United States Army, Camp Van Dorn, Miss.

1943–45   Employed at F. L. Jacobs Tank Plant, Detroit, Mich.

1945   Enrolled at Immanuel Lutheran College, Greensboro, N.C.

1946   Attended summer school at A & T College, Greensboro, N.C.

Returned to Immanuel Lutheran College.

1947   Graduated from junior college, Immanuel Lutheran College.

Entered Immanuel Lutheran Seminary, Greensboro.

1949   Graduated with bachelor of divinity degree, Immanuel Lutheran Seminary.

Married Jean McCord, Asheville, N.C.

Ordained and installed as pastor of Peace Lutheran Mission, Youngstown, Ohio.

1949–57   Pastor of Peace Lutheran Church (became Victory Lutheran Church in 1954)

1952–56   Matriculated at the University of Pittsburgh, Pittsburgh, Pa.; received a master of education degree.

Aug. 11, 1954   Daughter Jocelyn born.

1957–65   Pastor of St. Philip's Lutheran Church, Chicago, Ill.

1958–64   Attended University of Chicago, Chicago Lutheran School of Theology, and Garrett Theological School, Evanston, Ill.

April 27, 1960   Daughter Jann born.

1961–63   Pastoral advisor of Northern Illinois District Walther League.

Dec. 14, 1962   Son Roger born.

1963   Attended Lutheran World Federation Assembly, Helsinki, Finland; toured 100 other European countries, including Russia.

1965   Awarded a Lilly Foundation Fellowship.

1965–68   Attended graduate school, Indiana University, Bloomington, awarded master of arts degree.

1968–70   Assistant professor of education and psychology, Concordia Teachers College, River Forest, Ill.

1969 Guest professor at Concordia Theological Seminary, Springfield, Ill. (summer).

Ph.D., graduate school, Indiana University, Bloomington.

1970–87 Professor of education and director of adult education, Lincoln University, Jefferson City, Mo.

1973–76 Elected to Jefferson City area school board.

1977–97 Pastor of Pilgrim Lutheran Church, Freedom, Mo.

1977 Master of divinity degree upon being made alumnus, Concordia Seminary, St. Louis, Mo.

1986–89 Elected third vice-president, The Lutheran Church—Missouri Synod.

1987–90 Director of Lay Ministry Workshops, Concordia College, Selma, Ala.; taught specific courses.

1988–97 Guest professor in practical theology and special recruiter, Concordia Seminary, St. Louis, Mo.

1989–present Elected second vice-president, The Lutheran Church—Missouri Synod.

1990 Visited Lutheran missions, Nigeria, Africa; conducted an intensive course in adult education at Obet Idim Seminary.

1997 Guest professor at Concordia Theological Seminary, Fort Wayne, Ind.

1998 Guest lecturer at Concordia Seminary, St. Louis, Mo.

Honors
1965 Lilly Fellow in Adult Education, Indiana University

1968 Grant-in-Aid Research Fellowship

1968   Citation for High Scholastic Achievement, Indiana University

1997   Who's Who in America, Marquis Who's Who

Publications

October 1970   "What is Adult Education?" in *Lutheran Education*

November 1970   "Teaching-Learning Process in Adult Education" in *Lutheran Education*

December 1970   "Implications for Adult Education in the Church" in *Lutheran Education*

June 1971   "When You're Teaching Adults" in *Interaction*

1978   Homiletical helps (2) in *Concordia Journal*

January/February 1988   "Adult Literacy: Problem and Challenge" in *Lutheran Education*

June 1988   "Why Lay Ministry?" in *The Lutheran Witness*

1996   *African Americans and the Local Church,* Concordia Publishing House

August 1997   "Continuing Education ... Can Church Leaders Help Lay Persons Learn?" Commission on Ministerial Growth and Support, in *The Lutheran Witness*

Prologue

As you read this story, I believe you will agree that God is piloting me through a rigorous journey and even does the chief planning in spite of me. In these would-be retirement years, my planning is not exactly the "word of the day." I am not expressing displeasure. After retiring from my inspirational ministry at Pilgrim Church, I am continuously and joyfully involved in various dimensions of the holy ministry.

I have had years of involvement with multidimensional responsibilities. Each was propelled from a demanding circumstance. Several times I have talked with Jean about the phenomenon. "I often feel that I am on a continual run even into my planned retirement years." She has a well-rehearsed answer, "So you pursue the work of two strong men and wonder why you feel on-the-run." Then she can launch the previous month's itinerary in a few seconds. I have neither agreed nor have I disagreed. And whether or not the running has equated the efforts comparable to one or a team, I can truthfully proclaim that those years of full-speed-ahead, nearly nonstop, have their beginning in earlier years necessarily.

The story summarizes some of my near tragedies and/or adversities to which I clamor posthaste. At age 8, reenrollment in school is circumstantially prevented. Therewith the pattern appears to emerge in which opportunities with advantages seem short-lived, erased, or made difficult. Penetration of difficulty is fierce when I face death in a strange illness at age 23. Rapid recovery begins when I reclaim my childhood aspiration to study for the holy ministry. Survival of various struggles continue into future years. Some of my dilemmas are summarized in the forthcoming pages. I am including how my Ph.D. degree is nearly prevented at age 44. Later, after serving for two years in Lutheran teaching ministry, I am given an assignment diametrically contrasting with my original appointment to teach college-level courses.

The ensuing pages reveal how these and several other vicissitudes were adversities with sequential triumphs. You will notice that along with and after each episode, I am subsequently hurried into a wider and/or different focus of God's terrain. This journey is still nurtured with encouragement, and the fulfillment I realized in Matthew 6:33, "But seek ye first the kingdom of God, and His righteousness; and all these things shall be added unto you."

What follows are sketches from progressions (sometimes retrogressions) I have chosen to share from my milestones and mileposts, expected and unexpected. The events summarized are selected episodes evolving and involving my ministerial servanthood. In addition, the story includes scenes from life in my first family of 16 children and my current family in which I am Jean's husband and father of Jocelyn, Jann, and Roger. Seven of the members of my first family are deceased, and our three children are living elsewhere. But ultimately, both families remain very alive and functioning in my life. Some of this book's elements may appear unreal. My promise with warning is that all of the events and incidents really happened.

Immediately, you must visit my early years of formidable fortunes—the years that cast lifelong mirrors of reflections that travel with me. I am content to believe that God strategically uses those years to provide appropriate entry into His divine terrain, which becomes my unique racecourse that this book is all about.

Nobody told me that I was born into poverty.

1

"Sun" and "Clouds"

No Place Like Home

Papa says we'll be staying at home in Sunny South. I don't want us to move somewhere else ever again. I am six years old and starting to understand what really happened three years ago when we rode on a ferry across the Mississippi River to another farm. Everybody seems to know more about the quick move-and-turn-around than James (Jim) and I. He's the youngest of five boys and four girls and I am number eight. The others are Leslie (Les) the oldest, Leno (Jug), Zeola (Zee), Hattie (Hat), Carrie, Argestlar (Flemp), and Mary (Deet).

Papa likes to retell the story of how we moved to Louisiana for what he thought would be a better life. After a good year of 30 bales of cotton, and a really good corn crop, he began to feel he should return to Alabama.

"I don't know why," he would say sometimes. "It was a feeling, just something in me saying I should give up that good rented farm and go home to the land we left in Alabama." He says, "Memories of Louisiana just keep coming back to me." Then he stressfully adds, "A flood destroyed our house there two weeks after we moved back here." Papa also likes to say, "Leaving Louisiana was providential."

Papa pays rent for some of this farm, but all of us know that 62 acres of the farmland was given to Mama by her papa. It's in Wilcox County, two miles from here and still has a lot of woods. Our mule and horse must stay there. Papa told me, "It's against the law to bring horses and mules across a county line." We have two mules we borrow for the farmland we rent here in Clarke County.

Mama's big garden is not rented; it is some of the land that belongs to our house. Mama likes to say, "You children grew up in this house," and she zealously adds, "This is our home." She knows how to make a lot of good things grow in her garden. My sisters and I help her; the older boys work with Papa, and all of us help with growing the cotton and corn sometimes. Our crops always grow in four places, Mama's land and three other small farm places.

Tales by Uncle Willie

When Papa's brothers, Judge and Tom, come to our house, they are nice to all of us, but mostly talk with Papa. They are married. Uncle Willie, also their brother, is single and lives with us. He is like a loving big brother because he talks with us and does a lot of kind favors. He has bought Jim and me each an overcoat, suit, and other clothing. Twice, there were toys at Christmas time because Uncle Willie bought them.

He is often saying funny things for a lot of laughter, and he can tell stories over and over with fresh touches and twists. Sometimes, he treats us with a new story.

This is an evening cool enough to sit around the fire in my parents' room ("the big room"). Uncle Willie is telling his stories, some old, some new, as usual. We younger children are always eager for him to get started. My favorite character is the slave, Sam Nettles. "He outran the master's bloodhounds," as he goes on with the old story. We have heard this before; so on this night he gets my argument quickly.

"That's not true."

Uncle Willie looks at me, laughs, and adds, "Sam said he could run so fast he had to turn his head sideways to keep from flying."

His stories showed that Sam ran away often but was always caught. Sam Nettles made the chase last as long as he could.

"Sometimes Sam would go running through sage straw fields and throw down some red pepper powder while he was running." Uncle Willie said the bloodhounds were slower with red pepper in their nostrils.

Now my sister Zee is telling Jim and me that we should be going to bed.

"Not yet, Zee," I plead. "I want to hear Uncle Willie some more."

She leaves us alone, but she is listening too. Uncle Willie is just starting to tell his ghost stories. He has often said that he sees ghosts at night, and I think I'm beginning to believe him. Tonight he is telling more about the ghost man he saw who had no head in our front yard. Again, this leaves Jim and me too scared to go to bed.

We can stay up for a little while but must sit still and be very quiet. Papa has started his nightly prayer. He is kneeling by his bed, praying. We never hear him say one word. There must be no talking while he is praying, but sometimes we get tired of waiting and start whispering and giggling. Papa bumps his toes on the floor. Quiet again. A few times I think Papa fell asleep. I never told him.

Mama has a daily talk with God too. It's different. Hers

is in the daytime, and she just sings while she works. I think her favorite must be "A Charge to Keep I Have."

Mourners' Bench and Me

On Sundays when my parents go to church, all of us go. Today is Sunday, and I would like to beg to stay home. I dare not tell Papa and Mama that I don't want to go to church. Mama seems real happy to go to church anytime. Papa is a deacon there. But I have wanted to stay away ever since I was told to go to the front of the church and sit on the mourners' bench. I don't like long sermons. However, I dread hearing the pastor finish preaching because at the end of each sermon children ages six to eight or more have to walk to the front of the church and sit in the first pew. Adults sing and pray for us to join the church and accept Christ as our Savior. Some of the women even cry. I really don't know what they are talking about. The pastor always says, "The doors of the church are open. If anyone wants to be a member and confess Jesus Christ as Savior, please come." When Papa and Mama said that I was old enough to go to the mourners' bench, I felt good about growing up. But after the first trip I have been angry—just filled with dislike about the gruesome ordeal of sitting there. I am ending my trips to the mourners' bench today. I've been there for two years.

Here I stand. I have walked to the pastor, and I'm shaking his hand. "Yes, I want to accept Christ as my Savior. Yes sir, I want to be a member of Shady Grove Baptist Church." Now my parents and other church members are telling me how happy they are for me. But I'm wondering what happened. What does this really mean? What in the world have I done? I don't understand it, and I'm not asking anybody. I am told that in a few weeks I will be baptized in Cub Creek. My happiness today is that I will not have to return to the mourners' bench again, ever!

A "Cloud" until …

It really hurts. I am eight years old, just staring out of the window wishing I could go to school again. School opened today, and my ache hurts more as I watch the yellow school bus pass our house. The bus is for white students going to their school.

I am thinking about those two years that I did go to school. In 1928, when I was six years old, my sister, Carrie, my brother, Flemp, and I attended Kemp Grove School two and a half miles from home. There was no school for us here in Sunny South, Alabama. I was enthralled with school. I read everything I could and tried to read things I couldn't. Memory work and arithmetic seemed easy, even fun. My teacher told Papa that I was a swift learner.

Kemp Grove School was supported by African American Baptists of the area. There was no public school for African Americans in this section of Alabama. After a year of successful operation the school closed because there was no more money. For the school year beginning 1929, we were rescued by my second-oldest brother, Jug, who lived and worked in Birmingham. He gave us a Model B Ford to drive 12 miles on dirt and gravel roads to school in Thomasville. Now, one year later, Papa can no longer afford the gasoline and repairs for the car. So today it is jacked up in our garage. If only we could drive that car to school again. I wish it could be so even if the white students in the yellow bus try to spit on us again like they did a few times last year. Twice in one day I saw their bus slow down only when passing our car, allowing the students to spit on us.

I'm leaving this window and going outside. I'm starting to feel some wetness in my eyes. My sister is sitting on a front step. "Carrie, are we ever going to school?" She just sits still while holding a downward gaze. "I don't know," she finally answers. Both of us are quiet. After a moment she looks at me. "We might not," she says softly.

"Well, Mama always knows something." She is at the well, and I run over and help pull up the bucket of water. "Mama, are we going to school any more?"

She replies quickly. "Sure, I want you to go to school. I'm praying about it, and I don't know exactly when or how it will happen." Mama is much quieter than most days. Nobody seems to be talking much today. Around the table at dinner, they all look sad. Even Papa is hurting. He says it hurts him. He has told me how very sorry he is that our cotton made too few bales, and there is just no money to operate the car that Jug gave us.

Papa, Mama, and the older sisters are encouraging us to count, play math games, recite the alphabet, and spell some words. But those games usually played with vigor and laughter are getting no concern from me today. Days come and go as I hide tears and hold secret my wish to ride the yellow bus that goes by each day. I don't want to hear Uncle Willie's stories even if he still lived here. When he left to help Uncle Tom with the farm for a few weeks, I missed his stories.

Fall 1931. Our two oldest brothers, Les and Jug, take my younger brother, Jim, and me to Birmingham to live with them and their newlywed wives so that we can go to school. "I want my brothers to be edjicated men," Jug said often. "I don't want 'em to be like Les and me. I want 'em to be edjicated men." He always uses some repetition to accentuate his points. After three months at the public school for African Americans in Fairfield (Birmingham), Alabama, we return home to be with our family for Christmas.

2

The Good Shepherd Story

Like a Good Dream

On Christmas Eve I had my first encounter with a Lutheran parochial school when I attended the Christmas program at Good Shepherd. Sitting in a church, hearing Christmas carols for the first time, I am listening to the children sing "O Little Town of Bethlehem," "Silent Night, Holy Night," "Hark the Herald Angels Sing," and more. I'm hearing all about Christmas. My sister, Deet, and brother, Flemp, are singing with the children, too, because this is where they go to school now. The school wasn't here when Jim and I went to Birmingham. My sister said that this is a school started because of Rosa Young in Rosebud, Alabama.

The program is over, and I am just standing around watching the children, the pastor, and the teacher. "Rob!" Deet is calling me. "We have to go home now."

The four-mile wagon ride ends. I run through the door, ecstatically telling Mama and Papa everything I could remember about the program. "And guess what! I know what Christmas is all about now. Jesus is our Savior. Christmas is when we sing about Jesus being born. He saves us from the devil and sin." Now to my amazement I am finding that Papa and Mama already knew the meaning of Christmas. Unintentionally, they had never explained it to me.

It is January 1932. Jim and I are not returning to Birmingham. We are enrolled in Good Shepherd Lutheran School. A new beginning—going to school from home. And the phenomenal time I am having at school totally diminishes the six-mile round trip I must walk through the woods. The woods walk is shorter than using the road. The four of us walk fast and carefully up hills, down hills, jumping over small streams and crossing two creek bridges. Inescapable mud doesn't bother me; I'm going to school. Mary has everybody's lunch in one bucket. She gives me mine at lunchtime. I like the biscuits Mama puts into the bucket with sausage and the sweet potatoes.

Each day I am with the 35 children I heard on Christmas Eve and I am singing with them. I feel wonderful because Papa and Mama are saying that they know our new one-room school is going to stay. I am still a fast learner, same as at Kemp Grove, and already the top scholar in my class. But I am also trying to learn as fast as I can. Mama is sometimes talking about my rush to do my memory work and other assignments. "He works like that at school too," Deet is often telling Mama.

Deet and some friends at school are talking about some plans when school closes at the end of April. I just have to interrupt. "I didn't know our school is closing." Deet replies, "Not really closing. This school goes for seven months and opens again in October." Now I'm thinking. When the month of May rolls around, I'll be helping on the farm and waiting for school to start up again. But we'll stop the farm work on July 4 and go to the baseball game in the Baggot pasture.

Ball Game "Lost"

My sister Hattie talks about the baseball games, but she says that this is the big game on July 4. Her boyfriend plays on the home team. Also, two of our cousins are playing.

Finally, it is July 4. We are eating breakfast. Hat, Flemp, Deet, Jim, and I are talking about the game. We know Papa is listening from the porch when he says, "I just don't know that y'all should go down in Sunny South today." There is silence; I am stunned. Papa clears his throat and tells us, "I'll be back in a little while." Now we watch him walk down the road to Grandpa's house. We are starting to guess that he is talking to his father about the game. He gets a lot of his thinking from Grandpa.

Papa is returning. He comes to the yard where we are waiting. Papa looks angry. We quietly stand still and watch him walk towards the porch. He turns and speaks.

"Get the hoes; we're going to the bottom and work on the weeds in the millet patch." Hat runs a few steps to the porch, "But Papa, what about the ball game?"

"You are not going to the game. All of you, c'mon and let's go."

Uncle Willie is sitting on the porch with his head drooped. He seems to be feeling sorry for us. Papa looks at him.

"Willie, you come on too 'cause some plowing needs to be done."

At the millet field, nobody is talking except Uncle Willie. He is scolding the mule, calling it names, and really acting angry while plowing. He never acts out like this, but today, all of us know he is angry with Papa.

Late afternoon, we are back at our house, and it is no

surprise to see Papa make us some ice cream and lemonade. Infrequently, he treats us this way, and we enjoy it. Today it has lost its goodness. Papa serves the ice cream proudly, but we don't feel proud to eat it.

All of us know what probably happened when Grandpa heard about us. Perhaps he reminded Papa of the celebrative atmosphere at the Sunny South July 4 games, where many types of people mingle and while barbecue, ice cream, and other refreshments are sold, there are alcoholic beverages in the crowd also. But our thinking and talk among ourselves is that with Uncle Willie going, we would have been all right.

This day leaves me sad and with one happy thought: Joy and fun are around the corner as soon as Good Shepherd school starts again.

School and Church

Students enrolled in this school are also required to attend Good Shepherd Lutheran Church worship services and Sunday school. Papa and Mama have gladly committed us. We are Baptists and Papa is still a deacon at our Shady Grove Baptist Church. Now he is sending his four youngest children, three sons and a daughter, to a Lutheran church and school. Three sisters and two brothers are living in Birmingham and Mobile.

Our school subjects are geography, language, history, spelling, reading, health, singing, and religion. Daily, our teacher, Mrs. Chineta Riley, teaches religion and all of the other subjects, grades 1 through 7. Required and learned, are the chief six parts of Luther's *Small Catechism*, Bible stories, assigned Bible verses, and selected hymns from the hymn sheet. All of us have hymn sheets according to grade level. During the day, each class goes to the teacher for Catechism recitation and all other memory-work assignments. I am excelling in all of my religion assignments.

For the Bible stories all of the students help tell each story. Then, Mrs. Riley explains the story and interprets its meaning. The stories are from our "Bible History" textbook. I especially enjoy my religion class and singing.

My grades are always excellent, with scores averaging in the nineties. Deet, Flemp, Jim, and I are leading our separate classes with the top grades all of the time. All-school spelling bees usually end with one of us winning. On a particular Thursday, our pastor, Rev. Peter Hunt, is visiting and listening to Deet and me compete for the winner. He stands up and looks at the teacher and the two of us. "I'm calling an end to this spelling bee for today. I don't think that a brother and sister should be spelling against each other for a winner." Pastor Hunt always comes on Thursday afternoons to visit our school. On Thursday evenings he conducts the adult-instruction meeting.

We eat our home-packed lunches outdoors by the schoolhouse. We play games during the afternoon recess. For both the morning and afternoon recesses, boys with girls play jump rope, hopscotch, and other games. Only the boys play baseball and running the hundred-yard dash. After school we play games again before going home. On some days, upper-grade boys and older girls stand around, talking in small groups. Often their teasing can be heard. "He likes her," or "She likes him." Sometimes a "love note" is signed by a boy to a girl or a girl to a boy but only with the written words, "I love you."

Our teacher, Mrs. Riley, is also with us on Sunday mornings to teach Sunday school. Church services, Sunday school and parochial school are held in the same wooden frame building. For the church services, Pastor Hunt selects hymns that are also practiced and sung in school. I enjoy Pastor Hunt's sermons. He preaches in a different way than other preachers I have heard. I'm not scarified when I listen. His voice seems kind and loving when he tells about God's love for us. I sometimes tell Mama something that Rev. Hunt said. "The Bible tells us we are saved by faith and not by the good work we do," I tell her one day. "And that's the truth too," Mama says. I tell her it is fun watching how Pastor Hunt bobbles his head when he is preaching. I memorized one of the Bible verses he uses a lot. Bobbling his head, he says, "In Romans 3:28, we hear, 'Therefore we conclude that a man is justified by faith without the deeds of the law.'" Mrs. Riley gave us the same verse to memorize for religion class. I always look forward to Sunday. Therefore, my six-mile round trip is even more special. I am enjoying friends and cousins on Sundays even though I have been with them every day in school.

"Mama, Miss Riley is coming to visit us Friday after school." Our teacher visits in the homes occasionally. On this Friday, Papa is busy and not in the house, but Mrs. Riley is sitting in our living room and talking with Mama about the progress the four children are making in school. She makes other visits too, and sometimes Papa is there. "You have a real nice teacher," he often remarked. "She really knows the Bible and can explain it so well." And Mama never fails to brag, "Our children are just learning so much up there."

Mama and Papa always come to the festival programs and school closing. For one of the Harvest Home Mission Festivals, Pastor Lucius Means is the speaker. His text is Isaiah 6:8. Mama is extremely delighted and impressed. "His sermon was just so clear, and I understood what he was talking about, 'Here am I, send me.' He could really say that with so much meaning."

Confirmation

I am making a fire in the kitchen stove because I'm Mama's regular kitchen helper. She is cutting up the vegetables. "Rob, Mrs. Riley tells me you would make a fine minister one day."

"She talked to me about that too, and she asked me if

I had ever thought about it. I didn't know she told you."

"Rob, I'm real proud," Mama replies, "and if you really want to, that'll be real nice."

Then, very slowly I tell her, "I think that's what I'm going to do."

At school, Mrs. Riley had said, "Robert, you seem to really enjoy your religion classes and Bible history. Have you ever really thought about becoming a minister?" I told her that I was thinking about it. Later in the year, I tell Mrs. Riley that I think I want to become a minister. I am in the third grade. She begins to encourage me. "I think you would make an excellent pastor. Some people think that being a minister means living a sad life—most of the time poor; ministers may not make a lot of money, but the Lord provides for their needs. Look at Rev. Hunt, Rev. Peay, and the others; they are doing all right for themselves. After all, one goes into the ministry to serve the Lord and people."

Spring 1933. Good Shepherd will soon have its first confirmation of adults and youth. Mrs. Riley tells us the date. But today's date has a lot of importance too because I must hurry home after school and get permission from Mama and Papa.

They are in the kitchen. I check with Mama first. Zestfully, I announce "I want to be confirmed in the Lutheran church."

"You do?" she questions with a smile. "Henry, do you hear what Rob is saying? They sure have put a lot of work in learning the Christian teaching. They never would have learned that much at Shady Grove. Don't you think so, Henry?"

"Papa, will you let us?" I ask wishfully.

"I don't know. Le'me think about it."

Deet, Jim, and I are asking our Baptist parents to let us be "real" members at Good Shepherd. Flemp doesn't act as eager as we. He is five years older than I, and he is starting to talk about working and helping us three younger children to stay in school. Papa would on some days tell all of us to stay out of school for a day to help him with farm work. Now, when Papa says he needs us, Flemp interrupts, "Let them go on to school; I can take care of things on the farm." And he always adds, "There is no sense in all of us staying out of school when I can do everything."

The day after talking to Mama, we are waiting for Papa's answer.

"Papa, have you decided?" I ask.

"I think it'll be all right. The Lutheran people have done so much for y'all, and I don't see anything wrong with what they are teaching. We know the county wouldn't give us a school and no other group could keep a school running. Well, I won't stand in the way if that's what y'all want'a do."

"Thanks, Papa! I'll tell Miss Riley." Deet and Jim are as relieved as I am.

At home, every day, Deet and I are talking and planning for confirmation. We must wear white. Our older sister, Zee, is coming from Mobile for our big day. One of those busy afternoons, I am listening to Mama say, "I'm thinking I am going to join the Lutheran church too." From Mama, this is almost a surprise. Almost, because we all knew that she really likes going to our Good Shepherd Church. Papa says nothing about joining with her. He is still a deacon at his church.

I am 11 now. It is Palm Sunday. Adults and children are crowded into our little church. Papa, Mama, and sisters Zee and Hat are here. Zee is so very special to me. She was my "sister-mother," giving me special care when I was a baby boy in my family of nine children. She was 11 years old when I was born. During my early years, she often said, "Robert is my little boy." I am really glad she is here.

Pastor Hunt is conducting the rite of confirmation for the 25 adults. I am watching Papa's sister Lula Bell and her husband Lloyd be confirmed. There are baptisms today. My little brother Jim is baptized. Flemp, Deet, and I will be confirmed. We are all waiting for Pastor Hunt to ask the youth to come forward. Finally, he tells us to come. Approximately 20 young people are standing in a line across the chancel. Pastor Hunt's deep, clear, bass voice seems to thunder wall-to-wall, ceiling-to-floor of the church. He stops in front of each of us and repeats the same words. Finally, it's my turn. Pastor Hunt takes my hand in his.

"Give me your hand and God your heart, and kneeling at the Lord's altar, receive His blessing. 'Hold thou fast to what thou hast that no man take thy crown.' I now declare you to be a member of the Evangelical Lutheran Church."

The Wake-up Call

Summer, July 1934. Mama has finished washing the family laundry in late afternoon. "Let's eat some watermelon," she says. I feel real grown-up bringing the melon outside and cutting it like Papa does. Mama, Jim, and I are eating the watermelon in the yard when Mama attempts to stand up but holds on to the wire fence. Bending over the fence and trying to stand up she complains, "Oh, hm, oh! I'm getting as bad as Ma." She always called my ailing grandmother *Ma*. That is Papa's mother, and he calls her Ma too.

"Oh, oh." She sounds weak. Faintly, she tells us, "Run get Vola to help me, run get Vola!" As Jim and I help Mama into the house, she cannot walk at all, and we get her near the bed. We struggle and pull her onto the bed. Then I run as fast as I can the short distance down the road and distressfully tell Aunt Vola, Papa's sister. I walk home quickly, a few steps ahead of Aunt Vola. She isn't walking fast enough. If only Uncle Willie could be here to help us now. He has left again to help with Uncle Tom's farm work in Linden.

Tonight, the doctor is talking to Papa, and I am creeping near, as close as children are allowed, to hear what he is saying. He is telling Papa there is nothing he can do. "If the clot moves down," he is saying, "she'll probably be all right, but if it moves up, she won't likely live."

July 18, 1934. Two weeks have passed. Mama is still very sick. She groans sometimes and can't talk to us. Neighbors are coming to the house every day and taking turns sitting by her bed each night, humming hymns and praying. Papa, two sisters, Carrie and Deet, two brothers, Flemp and Jim, and I are feeling too bad to talk much about anything. Papa keeps saying we must pray to the Lord. We are praying and we are waiting. But Mama is just lying there.

About 9:15 P.M., Jim and I are napping on the front porch. A call from inside awakens us. My sister Carrie is on the porch crying, telling us "Mama just died." Jim and I jump up and run inside. My two sisters, Aunt Vola, and three neighbors are standing by Mama's bed crying. Elvin, my little nephew who lives with us now is standing around acting upset too, but does not really understand what has happened. Mama has taken care of him since he was born three years ago. Suddenly, it's like the world has ended. Now I am crying too. Mama is dead! Not Mama! No! She can't die!

Her funeral is held the next day because we cannot afford to have her embalmed. At the funeral, I am wishfully thinking through Bible stories how Jesus raised people from the dead. Wouldn't it be wonderful if Jesus would come right now and say, "Woman, I say unto you, arise," and Mama would be raised from the dead? Just wishing. I'm feeling some comfort listening to Pastor Hunt's sermon. "It is well," from 2 Kings 4:26: "Run now I pray thee, to meet her, and say unto her, Is it well with thee? is it well with thy husband? is it well with the child? And she answered, it is well." Papa had to plead with Pastor Hunt to preach the sermon because Papa's pastor never showed. Pastor Hunt finally says, "I will do it for the children's sake."

Two days later, Saturday, the comfort from Pastor Hunt's sermon seems to have left me. No Mama calling, "Go draw me a bucket of water from the well." No Mama reminding, "Go feed those hogs, and cut out that noise." No singing, and she really sang a lot while doing her work. Her favorite spirituals were "Steal Away to Jesus," "When the Saints Go Marching In," and "When the Roll Is Called Up Yonder, I'll Be There." And there was the old spiritual I didn't understand, "I Got My Hand in the Winding Chain."

I am hurting. All of us are sad and sorrowful. Papa is spending a lot of time talking with the four of us, but the days still seem empty—and the terrible void has me feeling just plain lonesome.

Uncle Willie is busy doing all of the work Mama did. He cooks, cleans the house, and washes the clothes.

"Now that I'm here," he would boast, "You all won't have to stay out'a school to do things. You know ya' Mama wants you to go to school."

Maybe I am getting a little comfort knowing that he is doing what Mama asked him to do, and I am remembering something strange. The morning after Mama died, Papa's brother, Uncle Tom, is in the yard talking to Papa.

"Early this morning Willie told me that Della is dead." Uncle Tom seems to be pondering.

"Yeah," Papa replies, "she died last night, but I just hadn't sent you word yet."

"I know," continued Uncle Tom. "Willie just kept saying, 'She's dead, let's go'; so I thought we'd better drive down from Linden and see what's going on."

Uncle Willie adds, "Della came to me last night in a vision." She said, "Willie, go take care of the children."

And there is something else I am remembering about that same day, the day of the funeral. Uncle Willie is crying. Papa and other relatives often said that Willie was the one person they had never seen cry—not even when growing up as a boy. Papa said that Grandpa would whip Willie longer and harder than the other sons because he thought he should make him cry. Uncle Willie never showed any tears.

Now I am remembering how when we were crying, Uncle Willie cried too.

One week has passed. This morning, Uncle Tom is back and he is arguing with Uncle Willie in the yard.

"But Willie, I came to get you."

"No, I'm staying," Uncle Willie answers resolutely. "I'm staying right here."

"Now Willie, you know you are s'posed to be staying with me now."

"Tom, you listen to me. I told you before we left Linden that Della came to me in a vision and told me to go take care of her children." Uncle Willie goes on talking, "You will have to do your farm without me 'cause I'm staying like she wants me to."

I know Uncle Tom wants Uncle Willie to go back and help him, but it is so good that he is here, and I want to hear him say more about that vision. In religion class I learned that God talked to Moses and other great men through visions. One day, when I'm with Uncle Willie all by myself, I'm going to ask him a few questions about that vision.

Later, Mama's brother, Uncle Sam, comes for a visit from Massachusetts and speaks frankly to Papa.

"Henry, you should have sent me a telegram at once when Della died. I would have told you to have her embalmed and I would pay for it. But instead, you wrote me and said, 'Della is dead and buried.' I would have had time to ride the train and be at her funeral. I know you couldn't afford embalming, so you buried her the next day. I could have easily afforded it."

Papa lowers his head and speaks wearily and slowly. "I'm sorry. I just didn't think to use a telegram." Then they sit in chairs on the front porch and chat. Later, I hear Uncle Sam say, "I'll be all right, Henry. We all loved Della."

One year after Mama died, Papa tells us that she had talked with him about marrying if her death should come first. "Your mama told me, 'I want you to marry a young woman, somebody able to take care of you.'"

After a few months, Papa announces, "I have met a real fine lady over in the County Line community 10 miles from here. Then he consensually discusses our feelings and his desire regarding marrying again. He tries to describe her personality and attractiveness. He adds with a smile, "Her name is Isabel (Bell), and she teaches at a small school." We are now wondering what she is really like. I am eager to meet her. But Flemp does not share any of my anticipation.

"I think it's time for me to get out on my own," he tells me. I had not expected Flemp to leave us so soon.

"Where are you going," I ask curiously. "Well, I told Papa I'm going to Mobile. But I did not tell him I plan to stay there."

"You mean you are not coming back?" I ask anxiously.

"Rob, Papa is getting married. I am 18, and I just think I need to move on. You will stay in school and be all right."

He certainly noticed that I said nothing. I know I will miss Flemp. It seems that he belongs here. I like having a big brother at home, and he will not be here when Papa's new wife comes.

I am 13 years old, and it is one year and eight months after Mama's death. We have been looking forward to the date Papa told us he would be married. This is the day.

Papa leaves home during the morning and returns in

the afternoon with his new wife. He introduces her. She is prettier than Papa had described. I am thinking that she is exactly like the picture of a pretty Indian maiden in one of my books. She has thick straight hair like Papa's and also has the Indian reddish-brown skin and high cheek bones like his. We have always known that he is mostly Indian.

We like her. But we are talking with her very little on her first afternoon with us. Immediately, Mama Bell is kind and loving with Deet, Jim, and me. She is a remarkable woman and over 20 years younger than Papa.

Uncle Willie has always been sure that we miss no days in school. He has been a great cook and has done all of the housework. As Mama Bell enters our family, he is outside most days helping Papa with the farmwork. Papa tells us he expected Flemp to return from Mobile to help, but has learned that he has a job there. I am relieved to see Uncle Willie helping. Papa does not know of the conversation Flemp and I had.

I am still missing Mama.

3

My Road: Into, Out, Into, and Out of Selma

Pastor Hunt to the Rescue

This is my graduation day at Good Shepherd School. Papa, my nephew, Elvin, and Jim, are here. Deet is at the Alabama Lutheran Academy in Selma. At home, I have a new brother, Henry Jr., who was born to Mama Bell and Papa. Today, Rev. R. F. Jenkins is giving the graduation address on Matthew 6:33— "Seek ye first the kingdom of God and His righteousness, and all these things shall be added unto you."

Dynamite! Is it possible that "all these things" could include high school for me? It doesn't look possible. High school means money; we don't have money. There are no public high schools near us. Before going home I am standing there pouring out all to him. "I hope your sermon means that I can go to high school." Pastor Jenkins said, "Son, if you really want to go to high school, the Lord will make a way somehow. Hang on to Matthew 6:33."

Pastor Hunt knows that Deet and I want to be church workers—she, a Lutheran school teacher and I, a Lutheran minister. He often drives his car by the field where we work. Today while picking cotton, we are not surprised to see him drive up and stop at the edge of the field. He walks into the field and speaks friendly as usual. After a few kind words with Papa, Rev. Hunt declares his mission.

"Mr. King, I stopped by here to talk with you about Mary and Robert going to school at the Lutheran Academy in Selma."

Papa's reply comes quickly. "I'd like them to go to high school, but I don't have the money to send them."

"Will you let Mary and Robert go if arrangements can be made?" Pastor Hunt asks. "If I can get them enrolled without asking payments from you, will you let them come?" he continues to question Papa.

"Yes," Papa slowly answers.

Pastor Hunt looks at Deet and me. "Do you want to go to school in Selma?

Our duet response is a quick, "Yes!"

"Be ready to leave with me Monday morning at seven o'clock." Pastor Hunt's voice is frank and very direct as he adds, "I am going to take you to school in Selma."

Relief! I am in high school! Alabama Lutheran Academy has seven boys enrolled, all living in one long room adjoining the elementary schoolroom. Thirteen girls are living in the girls' dormitory. There are three buildings, and I have learned that this academy is on 13 acres. There are two full-time teachers, Rev. Albert Dominick and Miss Delores Smith, and a music teacher, Mrs. Ethel Horton, who comes some days. Mrs. Lou Jenkins is the matron and the Rev. Edward A. Westcott, the superintendent of Alabama mission work, is our principal. I am having a good first year except I am frequently reminded some payments are required. Deet and I are here without paying the initial tuition, but $8 per month from each of us is expected. As my first high school year is coming to an end, I receive defeating news from Rev. Westcott. "You and Mary will not be allowed to return unless the indebtedness for this past year is paid in full."

To Birmingham and Back

In September, Jim and I go to Birmingham again to live with Les and Jug to attend school. Deet begins living with Zee in Mobile, attending Mobile County Training School.

Is it the school or is it me? I feel very displaced as I attend classes in this public school. As intent as I am on attending high school, I am feeling that it is wrong to say that I don't like this school. I am missing everything about a Christian school. But Jim's and my stay at the public school comes to an abrupt end, early spring, because Papa needs us to help with the farm.

In late summer I receive a letter from Rev. Westcott. I tear into it. He is declining the request I sent him to allow me to have a job and pay for my school expenses. So, I am writing him a second letter. He will hear a deeper plea from me—I am asking him to help a poor boy who wants to go to school and become a minister. Again, I am waiting for the mail.

My letter comes. Rev. Westcott is telling me to catch the next day's train to Selma. This is double happiness because I have recently learned that the academy has added the last two grades to make it a complete high school.

My job at school is shared with another male student— to fire the boiler that heats the girl's dormitory and the administration building. I am also making the fires in the kitchen stove, cutting grass, and serving as an assistant for the male campus students. This job is only paying $5 monthly, which means I will still be facing indebtedness at the end of the year. I need to talk with Rev. Westcott before reenrollment is canceled.

It is April 1940. I am a thankful man. Rev. Westcott is extending my job through the summer so that I can pay the leftover debts for both Deet and me. My senior year is approaching, and I have a raise. I will fire the boiler without help and continue the other jobs for $10 monthly. Jim has been home for a year without school and has made plans while doing special work on the farm with hogs and other things to earn enough cash to get himself into school. He will be here this fall.

This is already the most important year in my life. I have frequently meditated on Matthew 6:33. Today, I am finally nearly finished with high school rather than facing the dismay of not going. I remain the chief soloist for the school, but I have mastered more skill with my voice. Sometimes I am asked to sing from my list of favorites, "The Heavens Are Declaring," "Dear Lord and Father of Mankind," and "God Bless America." I am also realizing how fortunate I am to take piano lessons from Mrs. Horton and actually learn to play hymns.

May 1941. Graduation! I am graduating! There are 12 in my class. I am wearing a new suit bought by my three older brothers, and a new hat, shirt, and shoes sent from Zee. Papa, Jug, and Carrie are here. I am singing my last solo at the academy, "The Heavens Are Declaring." Jug lets me drive his new 1941 fluid-drive Chrysler around the campus. I'm impressed with his success and will ask my father to allow me to return to Birmingham with him and find employment.

I leave Selma and head for Birmingham with a heart filled with thanks to God that He blessed me to graduate from high school. I will be enrolling in college and a seminary in future years to study for the holy ministry. Also, today I am declaring that I will never go to school in poverty again!

4

Not Nearly As Planned

Plight 1: Employment

"No, we are not seeing anybody else today." I'm hearing this every morning while my brother, Les, waits in his car for me to stand in line at this Birmingham plant. He works a night shift but brings me each morning. I am now thinking I should leave and try Mobile where my sister Zee lives. Yes, I will leave today and begin a job search in Mobile tomorrow.

This is a great day for me. After six weeks of no work in Birmingham, I am working in Mobile at the Southern Kraft Paper Mill for a good salary of 50 cents per hour, $4 each day.

Fired, yes, fired! I have been on this job for one month. I should never have listened to a few co-workers plot against the order to crawl into the big sewer to clean it.

"Get in there," the foreman angrily yells. "I said move and anybody who doesn't can leave."

I stand tight and still with one of the chief protesters.

The foreman points to me and disgruntledly scowls, "Go up to the office and check out."

Immediately my protesting co-worker leaps into the

sewer and saves his job. I feel so very hurt and ashamed that I lost my first manly job. I cannot express the depth of my agony. Nevertheless, I get another job using a pick and shovel to dig foundations for barrack steps in Brooklyn Field. Hard work!

As a few weeks pass, I'm glad that the Lutheran church is still a part of my life. It is October, five months after graduation. Rev. Westcott, who is still the superintendent of Alabama Lutheran Missions and Schools, has talked with me, and today he is asking me to serve as a vacancy teacher for Bethlehem Lutheran School at Holy Ark, Alabama. I accept and begin the school year teaching 18 pupils, grades 1 through 5, in a one-room school building. My salary is $30 monthly, from which $10 must be withheld for college. I am able to live fairly well in a home with an elderly couple, paying slightly less than $14 a month for room, board, and laundry. But I must reflect. As I work as a teacher, there are the memories of the three-mile walk through the woods to Good Shepherd Lutheran School. I cannot forget those years as I now daily walk two miles through the woods to teach at Bethlehem School.

With the year of vacancy teaching ended, I really need employment. Today, I am in the employment line at the maritime shipyard in Mobile. When the employer finally comes out to select a few men, a spark of hope is quickly ignited but blown out just as fast. He ushers three men inside. "This is all we are hiring today." I am hurt. But I feel helpless for only a moment. Suddenly I am strong, and on my way into the employer's office.

"I am from a large family where my father, an older man, is a poor farmer," I tell him. "There is very little money for food and clothing for my younger brothers. I need a job badly to help my family."

The employer stares at me. "You are hired."

Now I am believing that I can save money to go to college because my salary is $37 weekly. Certainly, World War II is causing this shipyard to be a lucrative business.

Plight 2: The Army

Today, Dec. 19, 1942, I no longer have my job at the maritime shipyard. I have been inducted into the United States Army and stationed at Fort McClellan, Alabama. It was heart-breaking to leave family and friends five days before Christmas. Hurt.

I am very disillusioned with Army mandates. With two months of basic training ended, my battalion is here in Camp Van Dorn, Miss. I have been in truck-driver training for two months. Today I am going to my company commander's office for understanding and help. Another officer is leaving, and I can see through the open door that the commander is alone. I enter and make a salute. The officer asks, "May I be of help to you?" I begin, "Since childhood, I have always wanted to be a minister. I would like to work with our base chaplain or in some other area, and I am very willing to serve in any aspect of the Armed Services that does not involve me killing people or people trying to kill me." The commander responds, "Effective immediately, do not go out on the field any more, and do not meet reveille or retreat. You need not stand in line for meals and mail call." I'm feeling that this is a wonder of wonders, and he is continuing, "Report to my office each morning for assignments. If anyone says anything to you about your actions, tell them to see me." Now I'm trying to look at ease within my shocked body, and the commander still has more. "I would like for you to go and talk to the chaplain also." Relief! "Sir, thank you."

I am delighted with the first conversation with the chaplain. He is talking about his training for the ministry, and I am proudly sharing some of my early school life. Now I know that I must tell him about my aspiration to become a minister. He is listening and also commending me. I feel I won't forget how he said, "Godspeed!" Our agreement dictates that I have regular visits in his office. I will probably be with him at least twice weekly and attend chapel services on Sundays.

I'm feeling better about army life. One month has passed since speaking with the commanding officer. So why, today, am I receiving this envelope from base headquarters? Reflecting on my past life, the envelope could contain good news or other. Oh! I am being requested to meet with the reclassification board next week.

Standing before the board of top army officials, I know this is not a dream. They are actually informing me that I am being assigned to the Medical Corps under "limited service" and will not be assigned to combat duty. Relief again!

Two months later I hear an alarm. This Medical Corps is being activated for active duty. Again I am being requested to return to the reclassification board. I've been here before, but this time it's different. I'm here only for a few questions and a physical exam. Their focus and questions all seem to deal mostly with my left eye—injured when I was 11 years old in an accident while playing with a relative throwing a stick. I am told to continue with my Medical Corps responsibilities. This isn't college, but thankfully it isn't combat either.

One week has passed since my second trip to the reclassification board. Today I am just working and thinking while walking past the outdoor bulletin board. I stop because soldiers are surrounding the board and screaming, some jumping and running. A soldier bumps into me. "Sorry, I'm just so happy," he shouts. But a few men appear sad, just standing, and saying nothing. I'm going to push through these men and find out what's going on. There before me I see posted the list of men being honorably discharged. Missing names are the soldiers designated for immediate combat in Europe. The quiet soldiers are noticing their names are missing. I believe I am trying hard to breathe as I quickly read the list. I'm reading as fast as I can. My name? Yes! It is Aug. 27, 1943, and I am receiving my honorable discharge from the United States Army. My first stop will be Zee's home in Mobile to share the news before visiting my family at home and Les in Birmingham.

Plight 3: Detroit

College? Do I go now or later? I am reminding myself that training for the holy ministry is still my major plan. And I am remembering Selma. Therefore, I must not return to school poor.

"Les, I'm thinking about going to Detroit with you, but I'm just wondering, that's all." My brother, Les, in Birmingham is pleading with me to go with him to Detroit, where there are many good jobs.

"I know you will get a good job and can save a lot of money for school if you let me take you with me," he replies persuasively.

"Yes, I'm ready to go" I finally tell him. "But I want you to know that my plan is to get some money saved for college."

In Detroit, both of us like our jobs, particularly because of the excellent salaries. In the plant where I am working, tank parts are crated to be shipped overseas for battle. As an assembly line checker, I am frequently working overtime with double-time pay. College? Yes! Therefore, I am buying a nice 1940 Ford and some clothing for church. I am enthralled with the growth of my savings account. Precisely as planned, when I go to school again, I will not be in poverty as I was in high school.

One and a half years of financial progress and I am starting to ask myself how much longer do I stay in Detroit and where do I go from here. I am enjoying chats with the vicar at St. Philip Lutheran Church. We were schoolmates at Alabama Lutheran Academy in Selma. He shares my enthusiasm for earning money to go to college. I have disclosed that I may stay in Detroit and earn a baccalaureate degree before going to a seminary.

Spring 1945, but this is not spring fever. I am really sick. Today, same as last week, I am sending a message to my foreman that I am too ill to come to work. Two doctors cannot seem to help me. They each take turns guessing what my illness might be. Possibilities include flu, anemia, and low blood pressure, but I am getting worse. I'm going to my family in Sunny South, Alabama.

Plight 4: Dying?

The 24-hour bus trip has felt like a week. It is July and hot. The driver is kindly letting me off at the road that passes near my house instead of taking me to the bus station in town. My suitcase is small, but it seems to weigh 50 pounds as I walk the little dirt road towards home. Nobody is expecting me, but the family has learned of my sickness through a letter from Deet.

Here comes Papa, and I can easily tell that he is walking to his lower field we call the swamp. I'm trudging very slowly. He sees me now and is probably noticing how weak I have become.

"Good morning." he says politely, and continues walking past the "stranger."

After my faint "Good morning," he stops suddenly and turns around.

"Rob, son, is that you?"

"Yes, Papa," I reply weakly. "I had to come home."

He stares at me a few seconds. "Well, I was just on my way down to the swamp, but I don't have to go today."

Immediately, he takes my small piece of luggage and leads me to the house.

At home, Mama Bell and the five children are not treating me as a stranger. My new sister, Virgelean, and I are now meeting for the first time. I'm feeling good about being at home, worried because of my illness, and weaker the next day.

"Just stay in bed," Mama Bell is saying. "Get some rest."

She is using time to care for me as if I'm her only child. Throughout each day she monitors and cares for me like a special nurse. My illness seems very important to her, and she is suddenly a special person in my life. But I am also remembering that from our very beginning, when I was 13, she was a very caring and loving person.

My father's doctor is quiet after examining me. I am waiting for him to speak, but he is only looking at me. Finally, "Rob, I think you should go to the cemetery and pray." I am surprised at his counsel but too weak to get into a conversation about it. I'm not feeling the strength to talk. I am no stranger to prayer. I pray daily. I never prayed in a cemetery. Through all of my past difficulties, I have prayed. As my body weakens, I am getting no medicine, no diagnosis but more advice. Through Uncle Tom's suggestion, a voodoo doctor has a talk with me. He looks in his crystal ball and staring with big eyes says, "Young man, go to church and do something because you are a good man." When Aunt Bell writes me from Bessemer, she frankly states, "If you go on into the ministry like you said when you were a little boy, I think you'll get well."

This is my third week at home. My illness has gained momentum, and now all of my left side is paralyzed. A family of singers has serenaded me with beautiful Christian songs several times. Other neighbors have come and visited with me. This is like the peaceful prayer vigil they kept with my mother when she was dying. I'm totally bedridden. I am praying and don't know of anything else to do. I'm finally against an obstacle that I can do nothing to move.

Papa sits by my bed the entire night now. On this night, late, I hear him scream, "Bell, c'mere, Bell!" I am waking a little as he is screaming. Mama Bell holds my upper body in her arms, crying, "Honey, don't go! Please don't go! Breathe this camphor, c'mon, breathe!" I smell the camphor that she is frantically waving beneath my nostrils while shaking me vigorously. Papa is calling, "C'mon, Rob, C'mon now, Rob." I know I was in a daze when he called Mama Bell. He saw something was wrong just in time. I don't know how he knew, but I was really trying to breathe and could not even gasp until Mama Bell used the camphor and shook me. No panic jerk from me. I couldn't. My body was too lifeless.

One or two nights later, asleep or awake, I am having an encounter with God. A voice that sounds like thunder speaks to me three times—"Go and preach. If you do, you will live and there will be no end to your blessings. If you do not go, you will die and will have no assurance of eternal life." I am sobbing while saying, "I will go and preach." Immediately, I feel the transcendence of a healing miracle. Within three days I am walking with a crutch, but my feet are swollen double in size. Zee is visiting and enjoying the good news. She invites me to come to Mobile with her now. I am going.

In Mobile, I soak my feet in kerosene three times daily. This is the strange idea of an older man who heard that my feet were swollen. "Where did he get the idea?" I ask. But one week later, I'm not wondering. I'm just thankful that my feet are almost normal. I have to wear sandals but no crutch is needed now.

I know I must leave Mobile as soon as possible. I've been here three weeks. Today, there will finally be a move towards college. Regretfully, I can only spend two days in Sunny South, as hurrying seems mandatory.

In Detroit, where I lived and worked for two years, I am almost unaware of anything but my purpose. I have come to sell my car, pack a new wardrobe trunk, and buy some shoes that will fit my now slightly larger feet. But a few hours must be used to give some quick good-byes to Les, Jug, Deet, and a few dear friends.

5

Immanuel Lutheran College and Seminary

"Choosing" the Right School

I am determined to begin my college studies even though the 1945 school year began mid-September, a few weeks ago. This is Immanuel Lutheran College and Seminary. I certainly hope I have chosen wisely. My first choice was Concordia College, Fort Wayne.

Thoughts of Concordia College haunt me while riding the train en route here. While rushing in preparation to leave Detroit, I speak with the pastor of the Lutheran church I was attending and surface my intent to enroll in Concordia College at Fort Wayne, Ind., for the required pretheological training. He is emphatic with discouragement.

"Selma has not given you the background to attend the school in Fort Wayne."

He sternly reminds me that Fort Wayne is a white school with high standards. "You should enroll in the all-Negro school in Greensboro, North Carolina." I am surprised to notice that the pastor seems outraged about my choice.

He continues arrogantly, "I will not recommend you for admission to Concordia."

The pastor is also sure to have his vicar encourage me to attend Immanuel for both the pretheological training as well as my theological studies. The vicar boasts and reiterates the competence and preparedness of the professors. Then he talks of how glad he is that he went to Immanuel. I am still pondering the counsel of his bishop. There are other concerns too. That was my week of the rapid maneuvers of packing, selling the car, and other mandates. Today I am realizing that finally, but reluctantly, I canceled Concordia College, Fort Wayne.

Getting Started

Six weeks have gone by at Immanuel, and I have completed all of the work that I missed because of late enrollment. I am making excellent grades in my course work generally. Feeling the vigor to complete preseminary work early, I am considering taking courses at A & T College next summer. This will be walking distance inasmuch as its vast campus adjoins Immanuel's few acres. I have decided that I will complete the required 60 semester hours within one and a half years. Therefore, summer school is a mandate for me.

Semester II, spring 1946. God is daily providing courage and inspiration beyond my power to describe. Even though each instructor seems to assign heaps of work with various levels of difficulty, I am prepared daily. There is a very special lighthearted feeling about financial needs. The GI Bill and savings in the bank have absolved the return-to-school-poor. Occasionally, my thoughts cannot avoid Pastor Jenkins' admonition. "Son, if you really want to go to high school, the Lord will make a way somehow. Hang onto Matthew 6:33." Now I know that his statement includes college and more. Matthew 6:33 seems more important every time I read it.

"Hey, we were just by your room, looking for you!"

Three students from our men's dormitory have stopped me as I leave the building. One of them is inviting me to join them.

"We are just going out to get some food and maybe go to a movie."

I tell him, "I'm headed to the library to check on a reserved book!"

He replies, "Okay, we'll leave you alone tonight and catch you next time."

Another student adds, "You seem to be studying most of the time. You might enjoy getting out sometime."

I reply, "Okay, I'll see; thanks for asking me."

The three students are friendly, same as all of the people here. They have often talked about taking me places. Finally, tonight, they actually confront me. Like most of the other students, they are five or six years younger than I. One exception—four men near my age are theology students, married, and living with their families near the campus. Those students call me *King* as expected. But I am amazed that many of the other students and faculty unfacetiously address me as Mr. King. I have never asked why "Mr." for me.

Conversations about my noninvolvement with social life occur frequently, at least weekly since I arrived. It is typical to hear, "Aren't you dating anyone?"

My answer is usually "No, not really."

"You do go on dates sometimes, don't you?" I reply, "Sometimes." I am always able to tactfully end the conversation on the dating topic.

This year during the spring semester, life and outlook are drastically different from years and times before. I am applying most of my energy and time to completion of preseminary requirements. The dating that I have done in the past seems relatively meaningless. I am actually looking forward to perceiving permanence in a dating friendship some day. But I also believe that there is plenty of time ahead to seek that permanent person whomever she may be. It is clear that I am not a bookworm per se. I participate in the fun and laughter with students often. But I place limits on my time and will disappear to my room or to the library.

In the all-college choir, I am reliving the vocal music days that I enjoyed in Selma, including the solos. On some occasions we sing at Lutheran churches in nearby cities. Considering everything, I have not become a recluse.

Boy Sees Girl

May 1946. The school year is ending at Immanuel and four other colleges in Greensboro. I will take final exams next week and will soon begin my first summer-school session. On this particular third Sunday afternoon in May, friends from the men's dorm and I are indulging in a popular student pastime, walking through the campuses of A & T College and Bennett College. The two campuses are only divided by a busy street. We are among other young men and women in a crowded reception area of one of Bennett's dormitories when my friend Thelma sees me and immediately starts her familiar chitchat. We have known each other since last semester. She asks, "Are you visiting a girl tonight?"

"No, some friends and I are out just walking."

"Aren't you ever interested in a steady girlfriend that may result in a permanent relationship?"

"Yes, in the future when I feel I have found the right person."

"Point out a few girls at the reception tonight and I'll tell you what I think." After Thelma gives me a no-approval for two of the girls, I ask her about one more person.

"Oh, yes! She is real nice. You will like her."

Now I am watching for an opportunity when this girl is not in a conversation. The moment comes. We exchange a hello greeting. I give her my name and ask for hers.

"Jean."

"Jean, what is your last name?"

"McCord."

Conversation is starting slowly, and we are easily talking about most students' get-acquainted trivia: hometown, which college, the chosen field of study, and other easy topics. I talk about my anticipated heavy summer schedule, and I mention my wish to write to her this summer. "I am asking you if we can be pen pals just for the summer." She says, "Okay." When I request her address and begin writing, she gives each part of her Asheville, N.C., address as reluctantly as she has told me her name. She looks at me with a slight smile and says, "I must go now." I tell her good-bye and reiterate, "I am definitely going to write to you."

A physics course with lab is giving me more difficulty than my other course work at A & T College this summer. My other courses in my 15 credits are secondary education, American literature, and political science. After attending classes for a week, the diagnosis for a very sore throat and neck is acute tonsillitis; a tonsillectomy is performed at once. I am not going to miss any days in school, but as I try to attend classes, I feel extremely weak and the neck pain is almost unbearable. "I can tell that you are ill." My lab partner is talking to me after I told him about the surgery. He continued, "If you need to miss class, I will take care of our lab work and explain it to you later. You really don't need to be doing this lab. Sit back, relax, and let me do it." I am now thanking God for the "angel" He sent in the form of this kind student. He is also a veteran.

After two weeks, Jean answers my first letter. She writes a very enjoyable letter about her work at a cafeteria in

Asheville. She likes her job and enjoys fun with high-school classmates. My second letter to her is mainly relating school concerns and my part-time job. I really don't want to mention the tonsillectomy, but I am not well yet.

The summer session is over and Jean and I have exchanged three letters. The fall semester is only a few days off; she has not answered my last letter.

Fall semester 1946. It appears that I will complete the required courses according to my planned schedule. It is early September. I will take a walk over to Jean's campus and guessing correctly, she will have returned to the same dorm where I met her last semester. Right. We only talk about school and some of her fun activities and I am noticing how she tactfully evades the letter I was expecting. But as Thelma said, she is a very likable person. I can perceive an aura of happiness in her, and she tries to share it. She elicits a lot of conversation from me about my courses and heavy course load of 21 semester hours. As the semester ends I have only seen her once more. This is her year for student teaching out of town.

I am feeling both overwhelmed and overworked with the demands of my courses. Foreign languages have been my greatest challenge here at Immanuel, but I have held an A average in both German and Greek. In January, I will have completed the 60 semester hours plus a few.

Finally, the Theological Seminary

January 1947. I am admitted to Immanuel Lutheran Theological Seminary. God is worthy of more praise than I can give. I am traveling much closer to the ambition I cherished as a child at Good Shepherd Lutheran School. My professors are scholarly and very knowledgeable in their fields. Fortunately for me, Dr. Nau, the president, has already been my instructor for Greek. He speaks at least 12 languages fluently.

Now I am feeling compelled to complete my seminary training as soon as possible. No one is pushing me. It's my own idea. Two thoughts seem to toy with me. I am genuinely anxious to become a pastor, and there is the notion that I am late and may need to compensate for some apparently lost time. I am still reminded by some of the younger students that I should get out more. However, near campus, I often enjoy some time in the homes of some of the veterans who are nearer my age.

I have not had the opportunity to visit my family in Alabama since I left nearly two years ago, but by mail, we stay in touch. Mama Bell does the writing for Papa and always answers my letters. She and Papa have seven children now. My younger brothers and sisters are Henry Jr., Plessit, Adolphus, Doris, Virgelean, Iretta, and Janice.

On one evening I am listening to a middle-aged student explain to me that he is leaving the seminary. He refuses to disclose any reason, so I am trying to persuade him to reconsider. This is of no avail. I feel very concerned about his decision. Very late in the night, I am awakened by a powerful, thunderous voice, "Get up and read Romans 10:15." I had neither studied this verse in a class nor was I familiar with it. My bed is feeling very comfortable, and I want to go back to my sleeping, so I do and it happens for the second time. Then a third time, again? This time the supernatural voice repeats the command with a loud tornado roar that bounces me out of my bed. Whew! "What in the world?" I am wondering. I turn on the lamp and quickly lift the pages of my Bible to Romans 10:15. "How can they preach except they be sent." Calm repose transcends me. I return to bed. Sleep is peaceful.

Given consideration for vacancy teaching in a Lutheran parochial school for a year, a nontraditional vicarage is discussed. One day, early spring, I am requested to come to the president's office to participate in a conference with the president and three of the Synodical Conference board members. I am aware that this year should include a summer vicarage assignment, and upon arriving, that is the subject under discussion. After a warm greeting and welcome, one of the board members begins to talk to me.

"You will be assigned to perform your vicarage in Alabama."

"I do not want to be assigned to Alabama."

"Why?"

"I do not understand why most black seminarians must go to Alabama for service."

"What's wrong with sending black vicars and pastors to Alabama?"

"I believe God is too wise and just to send most of the black workers to Alabama when there are also other states with great opportunities for ministry. Moreover, I really do not believe the Lord wants me to go to Alabama."

"You will go to Alabama or else!"

Another board member intervenes sharply. "Leave him alone! Leave him alone!" The first board member responds, "That will be all, Mr. King. You can leave now."

I leave the president's office thinking that I would be expelled from the seminary. Later in the day, President Nau approaches me.

"That was okay, Mr. King, if that is how you feel about doing work in Alabama."

As the semester passes, I am hearing nothing about a vicarage assignment. A few days are left in the school year as Dr. Nau tells me I have an assignment. He is explaining that my vicarage assignment is with Dr. Carter, St. Philip's Church in Chicago. I am humbly elated because Dr. Carter is a famous man of God and known by many throughout the United States.

Chicago Vicarage and More about the Girl

First week of June 1947. I am on the train, headed for Chicago and enjoying conversation with my friend John Calhoun, who is now a ministerial candidate on his way to Detroit. Suddenly, I am certain that I see Jean on the same train, walking towards the water fountain, and she is passing us. I greet her at once, but she speaks reluctantly and ignores me. Later, here she comes again, glances at me, gives me a very warm hello. I feel somewhat bewildered, and my hello response probably shows it. Calhoun is laughing. "King, I think there are two of them. Check it out."

I am hesitating but Calhoun insists.

"Man, I'm sure there are two. Go into the other car and take a look"

I walk slowly into the next car and see two young ladies dressed exactly alike, wearing identical hair styles, and I wonder which one is Jean. I have not seen her for eight months. I am believing that if I approach their seat, one will smile as if she knows me.

It works. Jean proceeds to introduce me to her sister. They are not twins. Her sister is a teacher and came to Greensboro for Jean's graduation. Here is an empty seat facing them.

Immediately, I am enjoying conversation with her just as I did last year. She is still a winsome, friendly person. I am convinced that she is oddly out of the ordinary. I am feeling a force to ask her to correspond with me while I am in Chicago. She first hesitates as before but accepts. When the train stops in Asheville I watch the sisters leave while Calhoun jokes and laughs about the mistaken identity.

After arriving in Chicago and greeting Dr. Carter, he shares the letter sent to him by the synodical board. The letter includes, "We are asking you to accept Robert King as your vicar this summer. He is not desirous to go to

Alabama." Dr. Carter is smiling as he says, "I am pleased to have you as a vicar at St. Philip's."

The church has over 300 members with 50 or more children attending Sunday school. Early, I notice much vigor and effort for youth work in the congregation. It is very helpful for me to assist, learning more while doing. Seminaries expect vicars to be given maximum possible/feasible preaching experience. As my summer work is nearly ended, I have preached two sermons at St. Philip's and three in other locations arranged by Dr. Carter. My summer is purposeful and extremely rewarding. I am sure that Dr. Carter knows that I enjoy my association with him. He consistently imparts noteworthy, meaningful information to me.

Jean and I have been writing this summer. Nonetheless, as I leave Chicago in September to return to school, she has not answered my last letter. I am hoping I will eventually hear from her.

Finally, We Are Friends

This is a very important year in my training because I am scheduled to serve as the minister for some of the small churches in rural areas on weekends. I will be busy preparing sermons and will travel to churches using the Greyhound bus. On this Sunday afternoon in October, I am getting off the bus and there is Jean changing busses to visit her sister in Winston-Salem. As soon as I speak to her I mention the overdue letter. She apologizes and promises to write as soon as she gets back to Raleigh, where she is now teaching. Our schedules allow us to talk for about 20 minutes.

We are now writing again. Letters are sometimes two weeks or more apart, but we are still in touch.

December 1947. I am in Detroit to buy a car, and I make a necessary withdrawal from my savings account. Bus schedules are very inconvenient for me to easily get to some of the churches. And truthfully, I have really missed my car that I sold before coming to Greensboro. I purchase a black 1946 Nash.

In my next letter to Jean I tell her that I am now able to drive to Raleigh for a visit, and stated the date that I would like to come. She quickly writes to tell me she would be traveling on that day and asks me to consider the next Sunday. This will be impossible for me because I have a fieldwork engagement on that Sunday. After three postponements I ask her if she would let me know when she is visiting her sister again and allow me to drive her back to Raleigh. She accepts. Our writing becomes more frequent. I drive to Raleigh the few Sundays I am able to get away.

Jean and I seem to be the best of friends. She likes to ask questions about my course work. One of her interests is hearing me state the titles of the theology courses that I take. She declares they sound strange and has tried to recall them herself. I repeat some of them—isagogics, hermeneutics, dogmatics, homiletics, and exegesis. She has also asked me to explain what each is all about. Jean is one of six teachers for blind and partial seeing girls. She cherishes her work and talks excessively about the innovative ideas she uses with her students. I see some of the students sometimes because teachers live on the campus near the students. On one of my trips, a student asks Jean "Is that man going to take you away from us?"

During one of my visits in March of 1948 I propose to Jean. She doesn't seem surprised and states that even though she is 21, her plans are not to marry in the next two or more years. She attempts to give me reasons, graduate school first. Then I explain that I am willing to wait for her. I know that this is the girl I love and want to marry if it is God's will.

An Odd Vicarage?

Summer 1948. I am assigned to Youngstown, Ohio, to serve as a vicar for mission work. Jean is starting her master's degree at Howard University in Washington, D.C., and she is living with her aunt, her 12-year-old girl cousin, and her grandmother.

This is the last phase of my vicarage. There would be more but I am given vicarage credit for the year I served as a vacancy teacher under Pastor Henry Grisby at Bethlehem Lutheran School in Alabama. My vicarage here in Youngstown is under the leadership of the Rev. Walter Werning. The assignment is sponsored by the Missionary Board of the Lutheran Synodical Conference. Dr. Nau had been told that worship services are being conducted in a theater in McGuffey Heights, a rural suburb of Youngstown. I was also informed that two vicars have already served, one year each at this mission. As I arrive and receive information from the exiting vicar, I learn important facts about the area and the small community population. Surprisingly to me, worship services are no longer conducted in a theater but in the living room of a home. For my first Sunday, the vicar escorts me to the home where I will conduct Sunday school and worship service. The only persons in attendance are four children.

"Will there be more people coming?"

"No, this is all we have had for a few months."

"What seems to be the problem if any?"

"I really don't know. We did have a few more attending while we held services in the theater, but we were forced to move elsewhere and a friend allowed us to come here."

Immediately I express my disappointment to Rev. Werning, my bishop. He suggests that I try a vacation Bible school in the elementary school building.

I publicize the VBS by going door to door and displaying a few signs. One hundred sixty-nine children enroll for the two-week session. I recruit persons from the community to serve as teachers but time allows only brief preparatory sessions with them. God's blessings are even extending farther as I notice the church attendance increasing, with 20 children and 5 adults unfairly crowding the living room of the friend who is now beginning to express displeasure. Lutherans from other churches have become impressed and appear very interested in seeing a building secured. Through assistance from the Lutheran Women's Missionary League and the Lutheran Laymen's League, we are purchasing an acre of ground for a chapel in the McGuffey Heights area and also breaking ground this summer.

My correspondence with Jean is continuous, and I have gone by train to visit her once. I am now leaving Youngstown to complete my final year at Immanuel Seminary. William Griffen from our seminary will serve as vicar effective now as I depart. I am driving to Greensboro via Washington, D.C., to see Jean. We have had enjoyable times together ever since the bus-depot encounter. But she has not committed herself to marriage.

During November, the chapel in McGuffey Heights is completed under the vicarage of William Griffen, and I am feeling that I am especially blessed to be invited as the dedicatory speaker. Also in November, again, I ask Jean to marry me, and she gives me a reticent, tearful yes. We are engaged, and more specifically, we are certain that we are in love under God's blessings.

Two Blessed Events in One Week

My final year at the seminary has included special requirements for the bachelor of divinity degree. I have taken qualifying examinations in dogmatics and pastoral theology and defended my thesis, "The Cross of the Christian."

On May 30, 1949, my father is present to share the graduation blessing God would bestow upon me. With strength from the Holy Spirit, I still hold on to Matthew 6:33, which has very special meaning this week for two reasons: (1) Dr. Nau is conferring my degree, conducting the ceremony in Latin and Greek, and (2) Jean will be with me permanently. She is not present for the graduation, but is at home preparing for our small wedding, which takes place the second day after my graduation, on June 1 at 6 A.M. Jean and I had held lengthy discussions about a wedding date. She had insisted that if we would wait for one year, she would arrange an appropriate wedding in a church. But during our near-arguments about a date, I perceived need and strong desire to be married before embarking upon my first pastoral assignment, which has been scheduled for the third Sunday in June. This is also the date for which my ordination and installation are planned. I will be pastor of Peace Lutheran Church, where I worked during the summer of 1948.

Prior to our marriage we received the blessings of Jean's parents when I visited them during the Christmas season. I really like her parents, and they have shown real warmth for me. Jean's joy-type characteristics could have easily been derived from her friendly parents.

Jean and I agreed to ask my friend John Calhoun to serve as the minister to officiate our marriage vows. This morning, June 1, our vows are spoken in a simple ceremony in Jean's home. Guests crowd into the house with some arriving outside at 5:45 A.M. Papa is very elated to be present for our wedding.

Today, Jean and I leave for Detroit, where we will spend two weeks before traveling to Youngstown, Ohio.

6

Youngstown:
Peace Yields Victory

No Dreams Like This

We have arrived. It is Wednesday, June 15, 1949. The house that a church official has found for us is the home of an elderly couple. We are shown to our bedroom, and there is one bath to be shared by all. We are granted kitchen privileges with a cupboard designated for groceries and our cooking and eating times arranged between the meals of the couple to whom we pay rent. I am leaving most of my books in the car because the bedroom is small. We are only to live here until a house is found to rent.

The next day, early morning, I take Jean for a drive to see the church and to hear a wrap-up report from Vicar Griffen, who is leaving later today.

According to Vicar Griffen, membership consists of five children. I had baptized one of them at the child's request during my vicarage, and he has baptized four others. There is an adult inquiry class of four persons nearly ready for confirmation. Attendance for the Sunday worship is low, ranging from eight to nine people.

After receiving the keys, Jean and I walk into and around the small cement-block building. It is built well. But there is neither a lectern nor a pulpit. A small table has been placed where an altar may be in the future. Folding chairs and a piano are the other furnishings. Outside, an overdue concern has gone unattended. The old partially broken down barn still stands on the lot beside the church. Even though the church grass is cut, the adjoining acreage is filled with tall weeds. This is Myron Avenue, a short dirt street with no buildings on this side of the street except the barn and the church. The view across the street is one house between two fields of weeds. Three homes are farther away near the end of the road.

Until today, it was my understanding that after the building was completed, chancel furnishings would be acquired and the outside areas would be given some attention. It certainly appears that as soon as the building was placed here, church officials postponed or forgot additional assistance promised. Of course, I have received some personal attention from the Synodical Conference Missionary Board. After the officials informed me of the salary, I wrote the board and announced that I would be entering the ministry as a married man, thus revised salary considerations were requested. I am sent an immediate response. The board grants me a raise of $10 monthly. Now my total income, including housing allowance, car allowance, salary with no insurance, is $215 per month.

While telling Jean about my disappointment she asks, "Are there any church officials you can tell about this?"

"Yes," I reply. "I should begin with Pastor Werning, the circuit counselor."

In the pastor's home, his wife invites Jean to join her in the living room, and the pastor asks me to come into his study. Pastor Werning begins, "What is the problem you want to discuss with me?"

"I am considering not going through with the ordination and installation."

"Why?"

My response quickly summarizes what church officials failed to do before calling me as the pastor regarding the condition of the church, my housing situation, and the salary concern.

"You would not be here if the Lord did not want you here. Your call to come here came first from the Lord. You would be making a terrible mistake to accept the call and fail to go through with it. Your ordination-installation service is planned for this Sunday, June 19, three days away; invitations and announcements are in the churches and the newspaper."

Then he stares straight into my eyes. Determinately and kindly he asks, "Why not go ahead with your ordination and installation? After you are here for a while and unsatisfactory conditions still exist, church officials will see that you get a call elsewhere."

With Pastor Werning's admonition and the Holy Spirit's guidance, I am ordained and installed as a pastor of Peace Lutheran Mission on June 19, 1949. For this occasion the little building is crowded with at least 50 people. There are four black persons in attendance, including Jean and me. My spirit seems uplifted to listen and talk with many caring white Christians, and in turn, my spirit almost sinks as I realize I am looking forward to working among blacks in view of their significant absence today.

Prior to the following Sunday, I use each of the six days to visit persons in the church's community, inviting them to come on Sunday. Fifteen persons come. Jean immediately has to become our pianist. Vicar Griffen had given me the names of two Lutheran adults. Those two Lutherans with Jean and four adults are received into membership. There are many unchurched in this area. I know some of them and will make a few calls next week.

Stepping Out of the "Quiet"

House-hunting is an important chore this summer. Firstly, nothing is for rent, and secondly, my bank account has dropped to about $600, not nearly enough for a down payment on an average house. We are gradually feeling desperate to move. The wife of the man where we live reminds us to be quieter. "We could hear you talking again when you came in last night. You must remember that my husband goes to bed at eight o'clock because of his early-morning job."

She would usually continue by telling us how she regrets the situation but that her husband is easily awakened. Another problem faced is that carrying books back and forth to the car because of room space is getting very inconvenient.

On an afternoon in July I am rushing back to our room to tell Jean about a very livable house for sale by the owner. She arrives with me to see it and she is smiling, beaming, and talking about how well-kept the house appears. It is a two-bedroom, cottage-style house with shutters, a large lawn, shrubbery, a paved driveway, garage, and located in the city, a 15 minute drive from the church. The owner is a professional house painter. This is a frame house but really looks great.

As we leave, I try to find words to explain to Jean that even though I want a house for us, this will be special because I think it already has her personality. It will require a larger down-payment than I have as well as a second mortgage the owner is suggesting for us. As I ask Jean a hard question, her answer comes easily.

"Would you be willing to let me pawn your rings and mine and sell the car to raise the down payment?"

"Yes, definitely."

"Good, I will be able to retrieve the rings and buy another car in a few months."

A loan approval is nearly completed early in September, but we have no furniture. Sears allows a credit account, and we have decided to purchase only a bed, dresser, and a card table with two folding chairs. Jean has a one-unit electric burner her mother gave her for emergencies. We also have not opened the 20-piece cookware set given to us by her Aunt Sarah. A starter set of dishes from her parents is also unopened. Our landlady has not permitted us to use any of our items because of kitchen space. Jean insists that we wait on the purchase of a refrigerator for a few months. We can easily buy only the perishables that we will consume in one day. Her eagerness and enthusiasm for the challenge actually lighten the load. Both of us are thanking God for this rescue and the lovely home.

Jean has never heard my shrieking whistle skill until our first night in bed while we are lying there talking. I unleash my whistle very loudly. She quickly sits up and asks, "What is that for?" I answer, "It's my relief not to be quiet tonight." Now we are laughing and talking aloud just for the fun of it.

We Get a Boost from Caring Christians

Soon Pastor Werning comes to see us and our house. I am trying to show him that he is wrong to express regret that we can't buy more furniture now. Jean explains that we really don't care but he continues to express his bad feelings. Therefore we are not surprised that on the next day his wife and two members of their Ladies' Aid are visiting us and asking to talk only with Jean. They want her to know that we will receive at least one perhaps two household gifts from their church. They are asking Jean to list needs in order of her preference. I notice that they measure the windows. Within one week, a truck from Youngstown's finest department store is here along with a truck driven by one of St. Mark's church members. We receive new, heavy sectional shelves built the way Jean had explained with a corner shelf, curved end shelves and all unfinished as she requested. She wants to do the finishing. Also included is a durable unfinished chest of drawers, new window shades, and other items creating more surprises. The other truck brings a used oak Chippendale dining table with six chairs and table leaves in their own holder. There are two used soft chairs and arrangements to purchase a good used gas stove. Within a few days we are given a kitchen shower by the Concordia Youngstown.

During the first fall in our home we are told by an impostor furnace inspector that our furnace needs replacing. Without making any payment, we allow the Holland Furnace Company to follow the so-called inspector and bring a furnace. I feel uneasy and talk with attorney and friend Clyde Dyson who is aware of the group. The furnace is still waiting for installation. He tells me to hire a truck to deliver the furnace back to the company and instruct the driver to say nothing and answer no questions. I really like Clyde. He laughs as I report the job well done.

In Spite of the Bus

We ride the bus for transportation and I am able to keep up with the Peace Lutheran Mission work. It is November and attendance has increased to an average of 22 persons even though most of them are not members. It seems expedient to work with children. Therefore, on Wednesday evenings from six to seven, we are conducting Children's Hour with approximately 25 children. Jean leads their games and I teach the songs and guide them in learning and telling Bible stories. One of their favorite activities is role-playing and building their own dramas.

One day during this first year a member of the Baptist church informs me that her pastor told his congregation that some of the parishioners are letting their children go to the Lutheran Sunday school. She adds that the pastor is insisting that the children come to their own church. "I will keep sending my children to your church because they enjoy it and can tell me what they learned every Sunday," she says.

Finally, spring 1950, I am feeling the need to conduct a Bible class for adults on Tuesday evenings. They are attending well, but I seem unable to have them come on time at seven o'clock. After much pleading to please come at seven o'clock, I tell my little group that I really need to start on time even if only my wife and I are present. The following Tuesday, with only Jean and me present, I announce our opening hymn and begin singing while Jean accompanies me on the piano. Immediately, the door opens. The woman who walks in is a person that I had frequently invited to attend. She is now inside the church for the first time. It has appeared she does not attend church anywhere. The woman stops and looks to each side of the church. Her countenance changes; she seems stunned. She walks slowly to a chair and sits, but gets up and leaves before the song is finished, and just before our Bible-class members begin to slowly arrive. This is a very disappointing evangelism experience. She does not return.

Some Lighter Moments

Late spring 1950. We retrieve our rings and buy another car. The 1946 Ford is relief. It is more efficient transportation than the buses, and we are now taking children to Sunday school with us. The first vacation Bible school is in the planning stage and will be held in our church. The dates selected are two consecutive weeks early in June. We pray for success. Finally we are experiencing God's blessings in having a full house daily—about 40 children.

Later that summer I follow Pastor Werning's suggestion to visit a beach at Ashtabula on Lake Erie about 60 miles from Youngstown. I am using the trip as a surprise for Jean.

"Tomorrow we are packing our swimsuits and a picnic lunch for a day out of town."

"Where?"

"That's my secret."

"But I need to know."

"You will have to find out tomorrow."

I pack my fishing equipment. Jean is surprised as I park the car at the beach. She is delighted even though she is a poor swimmer. Her fun includes clinging to an authentic piece of driftwood she found. It appears to be a bad day for fishing, but just getting away is important.

Until our drive to Lake Erie, our breakaways have only been for a few hours. We had established a Friday night pattern of going to a movie theater recently built in a far-north suburb of Youngstown. There are some Fridays just before my monthly check arrives that we do not see enough money for the theater. But I always insist that all we have to do is look through the rooms and my pockets for loose change. We make these occasions a fun treasure hunt, and we always found enough cash. Finally we have a movie "kitty." Our other favorite place is a forest preserve park on some Monday afternoons. We pack our dinner, go to the park, and relax until dark or when the gates close.

I also get other relaxation and with productivity by fishing at Mosquito Dam or the Pymatuning Reservoir. We enjoy fish, and I don't mind doing the cleaning. We have purchased a refrigerator that has a large freezer compartment, perfect for the fish. Jean enjoys cooking the fish but does not want to catch them. She goes with me and carries our lunch, a blanket, pillow, and a magazine.

Early a Pain and Later the Vision

During the fall of 1951, I am rushed to the hospital in an ambulance. A severe stomach pain has awakened me during the night. I can barely move, and the pain is worsening. Jean and I are praying. We don't know what the trouble can be and the doctors are puzzled too. The pain lasts through the night; the next day I have relief after suddenly vomiting a lot of greenish fluid and foam. Now the doctors want me to stay for a few days so that some determination can be made for what caused the trouble in the first place. According to X rays, my duodenum is noticed closed sometimes and then remaining open as it normally should. A doctor suggested that the duodenum probably closed, being pulled by nerves, and had stayed closed until it caused friction and made a sore temporarily. But a neighbor from near the church has a different diagnosis. She explains that a disgruntled woman who wears the face of a friend is satanic and gave me a gift of a fresh pork shoulder that was poisoned. The neighbor warned me that she knew of the gift and that I probably should not eat it. Perhaps the doctor's diagnosis is correct, and on the other hand, maybe my neighbor is right. I am right that I really thought I was dying.

In 1951, I introduce the idea of a choir and begin with approximately 10 teenagers. None of the adults express interest, and these teenagers are in church every Sunday. I use familiar hymns from the hymnal which is also helpful in giving them more experience with *The Lutheran Hymnal*. When new neighbors who are unchurched move next door to us with three teenagers, two boys and a girl, we recruit the sister to sing with our youth choir. She already knows the descant to "Joy to the World."

January 1952. I begin to have a specific vision. Finally I disclose it to Jean. I tell her that I'm having an unusual vision of Jesus Christ standing in the middle of a certain street. His head seems to tower over the treetops. It is hard to explain; so we drive to that spot. I stop on a hill in an intersection near a store, in a neighborhood where homes are apparently owned by middle-class families. Neither of us recall ever being up there, and it is only a few blocks from the house with our "quiet" room. I park the car and walk near the middle of the intersection and tell Jean that this seems to be the area. I am gesturing with my hands and arms when I notice a dark red-brick building on a corner of the intersection.

"Jean, have you noticed this church here on the hill?"

"No."

"Neither have I, but I feel that this is where the Lord is signaling me to work."

"You are thinking that church is for you?" she asks.

"I certainly am. But there is no identification or sign anywhere on it."

"Some people are passing now, maybe they know," she replies hopefully.

Right! Later we knock on the pastor's door. His house is in the same block. It doesn't take me very long to give my story. He is very cordial and promises to let me know if his parishioners are willing to rent the church to me on Sunday afternoons at two o'clock. His congregation is Reformed Presbyterian. All of the members are Caucasian and the community is a predominately Negro population.

Several days, really about nine, are passed when I hear Rev. Wilson tell me by telephone that his officers approve the church rental for $10 per Sunday. I thank him, then immediately thank God. This is marvelous! I feel overwhelmed. Jean helps me with publicity and recruiting community residents to visit the church our opening Sunday. By the grace of God, 50 persons are in attendance Feb. 12, 1952, for this blessed opening afternoon. The text selected for my sermon is, "This is the victory that overcometh the world, even our faith" (1 John 5:4).

Sunday school is the emphasis at first, and we are already forming a children's Sunday school choir. They learn their songs in Sunday school and sing every second Sunday inclusive of their "Onward Christian Soldiers" processional. Jean is still our only pianist. By mid-March we are realizing a larger Sunday school than the Peace Mission. Second Sundays are especially well attended, as children bring their parents, who probably come because of the children's choir. But six weeks into working with the church and arranging the first adult-inquiry class, I am suddenly stopped for three weeks.

Pain Strikes Again

I am awakened one night because Jean is shaking me and asking me how I feel. She is telling me that my body is extremely hot. I sit up in bed and begin to realize that I have a fever, a temperature of about 103. I tell Jean that nothing hurts except the hard lump on my hip, which we discussed two days ago. It appears that a boil is developing, and we believe that when it softens we will be able to let it burst and handle it ourselves. Now there is no discussion. We are arguing instead. Our feud and fuss end after about 30 minutes as Jean persuades me to go to the hospital's emergency room tonight. Finally we are enroute to the hospital. I am driving. Jean has neither a driver's license nor the skill to drive. A doctor checks with me during the night. The next day I am assigned a room and told that an acute abscess is developing, spreading, and has not reached the point where it is ready for surgery. A surgeon operates on my hip the third day, and I listen to him and two other doctors agreeing that this is the largest abscess they have ever seen. Of course, Jean is sitting around waiting for the surgery to end.

When the surgery is finished, she is frightened by the open wound, wide and deep as a baseball, left to drain after the operation. The surgeon allows no closing of the wound and states that drainage must not be impeded. He explains how to use the extra-large gauze pads while I am recuperating.

After one week at home, walking is still very painful. For the church work, Pastor Werning arranges for both churches to have a preacher for the worship services. At the new mission, Victory, Jean conducts the Sunday school sessions for all ages of children in one class while the few adults who are attending sit and listen. The Bible class at the Peace Mission is being conducted by one of the members while Jean takes care of the children and teenagers.

Certainly my concern is the possible crippling effect my illness is having on the new mission. But as I return after three weeks I realize the Lord is demonstrating that my time out has been an example of His strength for His work. Thus, a reminder of my need to know that He is in charge, not me. The five adults at Victory have told me that they enjoyed hearing Jean conduct Sunday school with the children. It was their choice to sit and hear the children's lessons. The mission is continuing to attract children.

Two Churches and School

At the Victory Mission, late spring 1952, two adults are receiving instructions in their homes inasmuch as the church building is not available for evenings. However, there are at least 20 adults already attending services regularly and the Sunday school has at least 38 children enrolled. Such blessed momentum seems to suggest that a vacation Bible school is in order. This is granted! The Presbyterian officials permit use of the building weekday mornings for VBS at no additional cost. The two-week vacation Bible school enrolls approximately 62 children. Jean and I recruit children for the

VBS similarly to how we operated in order to open the mission initially. We employ door-to-door canvassing, she on one side of a street with me working on the opposite side. We meet infrequently to discuss notes.

While the Peace Mission continues with a smaller attendance than Victory, I am thankful that the members appear to be a strong and faithful group. I learned early that in the Peace community many persons attend their churches only sometimes with no particular reason for staying at home. It appears that Peace is blessed with an excellent Sunday worship attendance when considering the small membership of 25 persons. A Ladies' Aid of seven women has been organized. The choir continues to be children and teenagers and I am realizing that this is an evangelism strength. During 1952 officers are elected, a constitution is adopted, and we are blessed to be listed as Peace Lutheran Church even though we are subsidized, not financially self-supporting.

During the fall of 1952, with the desire to someday obtain my master's degree, I take my first course at the University of Pittsburgh, approximately 70 miles from Youngstown. Monday evenings are used for attending classes. Jean accompanies me on some of my test days and questions/reviews me for tests during the entire drive.

During 1953 God continues to bless both of the churches and my coursework efforts at the University of Pittsburgh. We are getting an evening out as often as possible. Jean is now working at McKelvey's Department Store, and the additional income is helping us to lay away some necessary items to begin our living room.

We have allowed the room to remain empty and entertained all visitors in the dining room and kitchen. Jean will not allow guests to express any sympathy about the empty living room. She is quick to tell anyone that it is her own idea to hold off temporarily. I think we are very blessed that Jean is an excellent cook, likes to entertain, and that we have a double-bed rollaway in the empty room. Already, there have been several times that friends or relatives came and stayed overnight and had given us only a few hours notice. We easily gave them our bedroom each time.

Prior to acquiring the used range, Jean has enjoyed surprising guests with an excellent dinner, including an apple pie that she prepared on the one-unit electric burner. This is a type of fun for her. She unswervingly hesitated to accept the used range we were offered for very low cost, but we accepted it with my persuasion. She wanted to wait and lay away her preference for a range, but I gave her my promise that her choice remains in our plans.

Talk about a Baby

On an afternoon in the summer of 1953, we have an unexpected visitor, the Rev. Meibohn, representing the Lutheran Children's Home in Cleveland. He said that he received information from someone that we might be interested in adopting a baby. I reply, "Yes, we are. We tried to adopt once but were unsuccessful."

Proudly, he states, "We have two Negro babies at this time, and we are trying to select an appropriate family for each."

Jean asks, "Are you talking about a girl or a boy?"

"I am talking about an infant girl that we have tested for intelligence and she appears to be so bright. We would like her in a home where her parents will allow her to have as much education as possible."

Now Jean and I are silent. Finally, I state that truthfully we desire to have children and for reasons unknown to us we don't have any yet.

"Rev. Meibohn, let us have some time to think this over. We will get back in touch with you."

"Fine, I hope you will decide to accept the baby. Before leaving, I need to tell you that we think she is a very pretty baby."

During the next few days, Jean and I are talking about the adoption opportunity but neither of us is certain. We decide to postpone making a decision and finally I inform Rev. Meibohn of our uncertainty.

A Vacation?

Early fall 1953. I have made four trips to Dr. James Miller to state that a strange paralyzing sensation in my chest and arms awakens me suddenly some nights, and I have to sit up and shake my body rapidly trying to believe I am not dying. The condition continues to return sometimes often in two weeks and later in either two or three days. Finally, in October, Dr. Miller suggested that I leave my work for one year and do anything but what I am doing now. This is terrifying news.

"One year? I can't see it."

"Okay. Try six months and let's see how you are doing. Also tell your bishop to call me."

Dr. Miller tells Rev. Werning that I am basically burnt out. He also informs him that he feels that my officials are lax in the support I have been receiving and that they are sitting back letting me handle a situation that is altogether a bad deal. Dr. Miller had learned that my efforts were not met with the kind of cooperation and financial support that other pastors in the district received for their missionary efforts. I had disclosed problems to Dr. Miller which are not surfaced in this book. A six-month leave was granted effective Nov. 1, 1953, with full salary paid. The circuit pastors would be sure both missions are given appropriate attention and services.

Jean and I leave the first week of November. After a month with her parents in Asheville, we drive to Alabama and visit my family through the Christmas holidays. We also visit my brother's family in Birmingham and friends, Rev. and Mrs. John Skinner, in Kannapolis, N.C., and finally, some time is enjoyed with Jean's sister and husband in Winston-Salem, N.C.

The first week in February I am feeling a strong inclination to see Dr. Miller again. Immediately, he tells me, "You look like a brand-new person. How do you feel?"

"I never felt better."

"Are those night attacks still occurring?"

"No, it seems they have vanished."

"If you would like to go back to your work, you certainly have my approval. I see no reason to stay out any longer. Now you need to take care of yourself."

As I tell Rev. Werning my intention he responds with a warm, "Welcome back!" Then he smiles and talks about the effective work that continued while I was on leave.

Still Remembering Matthew 6:33

I return to my parish work and continue to conduct Victory's membership classes in the homes of the interested families. During the following summer three families consisting of six couples and five children are received into membership. Four of the adults and all of the children are baptized on the same day. All have been attending regularly. Another family of husband, wife, and five children are baptized a few Sundays later. The every-Sunday attendance of these families is blessedly remarkable. Also, I am frequently commending their faithfulness and admonishing them to join me in hanging on to Matthew 6:33. They hear this in my sermons and in conversations.

I am given my second admonishment using that all-supportive verse. Rev. Luther Robinson's wife, Maude, is talking with me when we visit them in Cleveland. As we are leaving, she speaks to me, personally, with a radiant smile. "Be sure to hang on to Matthew 6:33." A few months later I am the preacher for her funeral.

Realizing the needed advantage of Victory owning a building, I must approach Rev. Wilson and let him know that if his congregation should decide to sell their building, I would like him to offer the first opportunity to Victory. He promises we will be the first that he informs. At the end of March 1954 the Reformed Presbyterian Church officials are ready to sell their building, and the Lutheran district officials are immediately cooperative in negotiating and purchasing the building for $21,000. Peace Lutheran members are transferring to Victory, and the Peace building is sold.

Now we are inheriting a problem that seemed to have gone unattended while we were renting. Men drinking from bottles in paper bags are loitering on the church steps in the late afternoon. As I begin to finally talk with them, inviting them inside, they seem to be disappearing. A neighbor tells me that when the men see my car approaching from a distance, they run. Some of the neighbors are laughing at the comedy. Finally, the men and their bottles are never seen on the steps. One who later returned alone has accepted my invitation to come to our New Year's Eve service.

Aug. 11, 1954. Our first child is born, a daughter, Jocelyn. The congregation seems extremely enthusiastic about her and is buying a washing machine for us. Now we are realizing how we nearly had two babies, perhaps. We had decided to call Rev. Meibohn and tell him that if "our" little girl is still there we will make adoption arrangements in May. Then we learn that Jean is pregnant, and we must cancel the adoption idea. However, when the children's home representatives come to Youngstown in July, Jean asks about the baby. The child has been adopted in June.

Finally, an adult choir is begun and a new member will

play the piano. I direct the choir in SATB music. Jean continues with the Sunday school choir, which is proving to be motivational for adults as well as the children. Unchurched parents of these children gradually, slowly, decide to take the adult-instruction classes. Our Walther League is organized with eight youth. There is a Cub Scout Pack with two den mothers and a scout master. Jean is one of the den mothers temporarily.

After procedures including preparation of a constitution are accomplished, the mission becomes officially incorporated. The next necessities are the building of a chancel and an outdoor sign. When filled, the building accommodates approximately 136 persons. Dedication is held in November of 1954, with my schoolmate, Rev. O. R. Thompson as the speaker.

In 1955 the work in the neighborhoods surrounding the church is blessed with a steady but slow increase in attendance for Sunday school and the worship service. These visitors include some new ones and some returning. It is suddenly apparent that most of our members need more sensitivity to the evangelism potential that is inherent in friendliness shown to visitors. It now seems appropriate to conduct a few informal member-only discussions regarding visitors. Simultaneously, some of the members begin following through by showing more friendliness and also contacting the unchurched visitors. Then there are gratifying scenes of a few members bringing visitors with them.

We Move Closer to Victory, but We Leave

This same year, I notice that the house next door to the church is for sale. Even though we live only three miles from the church, I am feeling inclined to live beside the church and facilitate more weekday use of the building while living in the heart of its geographic community. Renting our house is easy. Interested persons had previously asked to be notified if we should ever want to sell. We sell the house eventually.

The house beside the church needs a total interior/exterior paint attention, and its large yard seems to have never had a lawn. It is in need of measuring up to our satisfaction and to other houses on this street. One of our members is able to provide tremendous assistance with the painting.

My work in Youngstown allowed me to be attracted to fellow Lutherans in Ontario, Canada, through Pastor Phillip Fiess. I made four preaching trips between 1952 and 1957, Petawawa, Locksley, and Stratford. When the Locksley elders held a conference with me regarding extending me a call, I told them I felt I should remain in the U.S. central states currently. Jean and I have enjoyed stretching each annual trip into a week of vacation in Canada. Our favorite is stopping at Grimsby Beach in Ontario, where the cabins on the lakefront are very inexpensive. There is neither hot water nor telephone but the "getaways" are refreshing. After Jocelyn is born, we include her too.

A day in June 1956, Jean goes with me to the University of Pittsburgh to attend the commencement as I receive my master of education degree. I had prayed for this success and now I am thanking God that it finally happened. I earned the degree in religious education.

Fall 1956. Jean is given a teaching position at Hillman Junior High School. The Youngstown Board of Education lifts its 25 year ban on giving contracts to married women, and Jean receives the position immediately. We need this additional income and fortunately a member of our congregation will be caring for Jocelyn in our home.

In the spring of 1957 the membership of Victory is 175. One hundred are youth and adult members. But I am not to continue as the pastor of this congregation.

During August I receive a call to St. Philip's Lutheran Church to succeed Dr. Marmaduke Carter. I have received calls before and returned them, but I am already feeling different about this one. After two weeks and serious prayer, I write a letter of acceptance. I have discussed it with Jean, and both of us feel that it is God's will that I go to St. Philip's. Jean discloses that she has a slight inhibition about living in Chicago.

7

Succeeding Dr. Carter

Thoughts

Friday afternoon, November 1, we are driving through suburban Chicago, gradually approaching the center of the city, where I will become the pastor of St. Philip's Church. My thoughts of this future step are not pondered without the interjection of emotions I experienced while preparing to say farewell to Victory. Certainly when I received the call, I felt inclined to come to St. Philip's Church because it appeared that the Lord was beckoning. There I was in Youngstown, no longer facing the expected and unexpected problems in establishing a church, but serving the now-thriving congregation that God used me to plant. I was rejoicing over the vigorous participation of the members. Strategic planning was occurring with the Victory congregation and me. But the officers at St. Philip's Church seemed to have been hurrying. They asked me to allow the installation immediately as possible. Then I knew that I would not be with Victory congregation for one more Advent and Christmas for which I was already preparing. Jean is remaining with her teaching position until December. Also, she will be handling the work needed to be done in our house before closing it. Therefore she and Jocelyn are returning to Youngstown after the installation. Within a few weeks, I will return to Youngstown to do some of the difficult chores in the house. I am aware that in spite of me God is conducting this move—and much earlier than I would have foolishly guessed.

Upon my arrival at Dr. Carter's residence in Chicago, his handshake and smile are equally warm, and I feel a fatherly kinship as we embrace.

"I am extremely pleased that you accepted the call to be the pastor of St. Philip's Church. I am too old to care for the flock as I would like to. We need a young man like you."

"Dr. Carter, I really consider it an honor to be your successor. I have been thinking about my vicarage with you 10 years ago. Before I left Chicago in 1947, I dreamed that if it would be the Lord's will, I would certainly like to return and be the pastor of St. Philip's, succeeding you."

"And I want you to know that you will be the pastor and not a vicar under my care as you were 10 years ago. You will be the pastor. The voters' assembly has unanimously made me the honorary pastor—whatever that means. I guess it is some kind of honor bestowed on me because I was the congregation's founder and their only pastor for 33 years."

Dr. Carter pauses for a few seconds, performs his famous rubbing and wringing of his hands, and continues, "I made it clear that Rev. King will be the pastor and I do not plan to be in his way."

"Thank you for your kind words. Of course, you know I'll be expecting your wisdom and counsel, which will always be appreciated. You are still needed. All of us know this is Chicago's mother congregation."

Installation with the Carter "Touch"

Nov. 3, 1957, 3 P.M. Dr. Carter is the officiant for the installation service with my Immanuel colleague, Rev.

Howard Foard, serving as liturgist and the sermon given by the Rev. Edgar Robinson. The rite of installation ends, Dr. Carter comes and stands beside me; two elders come forward. They lift Dr. Carter's stole from his shoulders and place it around my neck. I am feeling a wonder of astonishment and must certainly talk with Dr. Carter about the surprise. Prior to the recession, St. Philip's 20-voice choir sings a resounding performance of Handel's "Hallelujah Chorus."

At my first opportunity I surface my inquiry about the stole. "Dr. Carter, what is meant by the action taken with your stole during the service—from your neck to mine?"

His clear bass voice was powerful. "That is to signify to the congregation I am turning over the pastoral roles and functions of St. Philip's Lutheran Church to you, willingly and voluntarily after 33 years of my work."

A Surprise Challenge

Because the church is filled, standing room only for the installation, it appears that overall participation is still as strong as it was in 1947. This appearance is short-lived, as I come to the church the next week for my first Sunday as pastor and walk through the Sunday school area that was so filled with children 10 years ago. Today, I see nine children in the Sunday school. The superintendent is with me. I tell him, "This is probably a once-in-a-while low attendance."

"No, this is all we have now."

"Perhaps I'm standing here remembering the larger group 10 years ago."

"Well, we just don't have any more than this."

"Who is working with them for a children's Christmas program?"

"That's something I need to tell you. We have canceled having a children's program this year because there are so few children."

The conversation ends. I have heard alarming news and will be doing some thinking, prayerfully and carefully. Additional not-so-good news is that I learn that many of the members are neglecting to bring or send their children to Sunday school.

God blesses my first efforts. I admonish parents during the sermons and informally after church. Children are trickling in on Sundays. However, I am informed that a Christmas program still remains canceled. I am thankful that Jean will be here the first week of December. The two of us are experienced. We can recruit and rehearse for a program simultaneously.

Upon my request, Jean develops a simple and meaningful children's service of carols, Scripture to be read by two teenage boys, who are first cousins, and a Nativity scene. Part of the Sunday school hour can be used for rehearsing. The Women's Auxiliary takes notice and gives serious assistance. More specifically, they ask Jean to tell them anything that she would like them to do. They dress the children like a Christmas choir, large red bows on white shirts, and provide candles for their processional. The service ends with a filled church in attendance. A repeated question is, "How did you get all of those children?" Approximately 45 children are participants. God is re-enlivening His Sunday school at St. Philip's.

The Unique Parsonage

Our appointed home is a large three-bedroom apartment on the second floor of the two-story apartment building previously owned by Dr. Carter. The church is in the process of buying the property from him. The once-beautiful woodwork and the quality hardwood floors are all in need of crucial restoration. We can imagine much potential, but Jean feels bewildered to plan the make-over without professional help. So she sketches the floor plan and consults a free interior service at Carson Pirie Scott & Co. The church is cooperative in following through inclusive of woodwork, walls, floor sanding, and rebuilding a room to accommodate books and a desk for my study. Very early, the place is transformed into a beautiful home.

Dr. Carter and Jocelyn

Immediately, Dr. Carter and his wife, Hazel, are loving friends for us, and they are showing a special warm liking for Jocelyn, age 3. Until we arrived, the only tenant on this second floor was one quiet adult for 15 years. Now after a few weeks, Dr. Carter is boasting about the sounds he hears overhead. Hazel likes to assure us that he is very sincere about enjoying Jocelyn's sounds, her indoor skates, the dog, and all. Dr. Carter expects Jocelyn to visit him two or more times weekly. Already they are buddies. For nearly every visit, Jocelyn asks, "Dr. Carter, do you want to see me do a stunt?" He answers, "Yes, Jocelyn. I would like to see you do a stunt." She places hands and feet on the floor, raises one foot and says, "Dr. Carter, I'm doing a stunt." He always gives his compliment, "Good, Jocelyn! You did a stunt." Then he adds, "She is a copious child."

Later in the winter he makes his first trip upstairs and wants to see Jocelyn. Dr. and Mrs. Carter ring our doorbell, and are standing at the bottom of the steps. Mrs. Carter announces, "We haven't heard Jocelyn yesterday or today." We tell them that she is ill.

Standing by her bed, they are silent. Dr. Carter's countenance changes and he, himself, begins to look ill. Jocelyn's body makes a sharp jerk with each gasp for breath during an asthmatic bronchitis attack. Her hard breathing is like the sound of a horn. She cannot talk. Her eyes focus on the Carters, and they only stare at her. We try to clarify that she has always had the attacks several weeks apart. Dr. Carter remains silent and lets Hazel talk briefly before leaving, as he only says "I'm so sorry." The following day, Hazel informs us that her husband was very shaken to see Jocelyn and that he just wasn't himself the remainder of the day. Certainly, Jocelyn's next visit downstairs is a celebration.

Some Concerns between the Congregation and Me

Succeeding Dr. Carter is a meaningful family friendship, but more specifically, it indicates my earnest commitment in assuming the responsibilities at St. Philip's Church, a very unusual and unique congregation. One uniqueness of this congregation is both interesting and important to me. The talent among the members is amazing and the dormancy of much of this talent is equally amazing, especially in view of some of the areas needing help. In contrast to the Youngstown experience, my efforts here are not aimed toward establishing a congregation in a place with great potential. In Chicago, I am guiding faithful members to realize their great, God-given potentials towards accomplishing work in an established congregation.

There are carpenters and a construction foreman who are responding to my call to alleviate the condition of crumbling steps outside the church building and broken pews standing in the rear of the undercroft. Nine to 12 faithful members who are public-school teachers, with my encouragement, conduct the first vacation Bible school with approximately 75 children for two weeks. They work extremely well together and appear to have no problems with organization or the children.

The head usher and assistants are well organized, alert, and industrious. They are cooperative and in full compliance with my direction to establish more necessary order for how worshipers conduct themselves in entering and leaving.

Serious evangelism willingness is apparent. Thirty persons assemble for training and participation in St. Philip's first canvass of its neighborhood. This effort appears to spark more interest in my continuous evangelism thrust. Fruits of these labors are visible as the attendance grows along with a larger youth confirmation class and more adults enrolled for instruction.

Most of the members have good to excellent incomes. The chairman of the congregation and elders eagerly approve my request to conduct my own brief fund-raising activity to pay the balance of the parsonage debt. This indebtedness is being paid slowly from volunteer contributions.

My task is easy. After a worship service, I announce, "In the next few weeks I will visit members I know can afford a generous contribution. Therefore, for each of you with whom I make an appointment, I am expecting a contribution of at least $100." It is interesting to consider the welcome and warmth with which I am received for each visit along with apparent eagerness to contribute to the fund.

The mortgage for the remaining $5,000 is burned in a brief ceremony with much relief. Other than this situation, I am having no desire to conduct fund-raising for the church.

I continue to be pleased with the good musicianship and quality of the adult choir. Some of the anthems used were also sung in our choir at Immanuel College. I am in my fourth year at St. Philip's when I gladly accept the director's invitation to join the tenor section for "The Seven Last Words of Christ" cantata. I continue to sing with the choir on various occasions.

During my forthcoming years at St. Philip's, I guide members into areas in which some training and gradual growth are important. (1) An evangelism committee will continue the early thrust made during my first year. (2) A stewardship focus will give emphasis from a selected group who would consider time, talents, and financial resources. (3) Bible classes, Sunday school and vacation Bible school are to receive direction and assistance from the newly formed Christian Education Committee. (4) Initiating the church's Lutheran Women's Missionary League (LWML) will help St. Philip's have a global church-body perspective. The women have a vigorous start with Mrs. Josephine Dilworth, Mrs. Bea Huff, and Mrs. Martha Tyler. The Men's Club, the church's arm for the Lutheran Laymen's League (LLL), is gradually developing more vitality than previously.

The Family Night concept that I used successfully in Youngstown is now implemented and enjoyed at St. Philip's. These are advantageous moments for adults, youth, and children having good times with games, singing, guitars, poetry reading, fun things, and supper.

An Inside-the-Family Update

During the second summer in Chicago, Ellen, Jean's sister is with us for a while. "Aunt Ellen" and Jocelyn are real pals. We need a person to be with Jocelyn for some of our weekends away. A visit from her is a delightful treat for all of us. Another trip to Canada has been a strong desire since coming to Chicago. All of us, including Snowball, our black cocker spaniel, take the trip. The dog is a gift to Jean from me in Youngstown. His "snowball" is only visible when we push back the thick black hair on his chest. We rent a double cabin on Nottawasaga Bay in Ontario. Certainly, fishing is planned. But on my first day's attempt my three ladies' enjoyable stone-throwing to watch ripples had to be moved much farther downstream. Their fun is incompatible with mine. The trip accomplishes my intent, a getaway with safe relaxation where our dog is enjoyed instead of being left in a kennel.

The following spring we have a very special family blessing. Our daughter, Jann, is born on April 27, 1960. Jean attempts to sit on a rear seat with her in church just as she did when Jocelyn was an infant. But Jann cries spasmodically. The problem is solved when an observant member tells Jean that Jann only fusses each time she hears me talk. Therefore, Jann becomes a member of the church's nursery on Sundays. Within two months after her birth, our pediatrician discovers a major crippling disease developing with her thigh and hip socket. We continuously praise and thank God that an orthopedic surgeon was able to obtain a perfect correction by having Jann strapped into a pillow splint for one and one-half years, followed with special shoes and annual X rays through age 6.

Youth Action: St. Philip's and Beyond

In 1960 the largest youth confirmation class, 14 young teenagers enrolls for the two-year confirmation study on Saturday mornings. They are not eligible for the Walther League, but I believe they may benefit from enjoying games and snacks together after class on Saturdays. These teenagers and their parents welcome this idea. Jean comes to the church to conduct the after-class activities, which is not at all a chore for her. When I ask her help she is eager, as I expected. I feel that I should note that Jean's adaptation to working with teenagers is a natural characteristic. She has told me that during her freshman year in college, a Presbyterian school, she received training in youth leadership with an emphasis in leading outdoor worship. She says that while taking the course, she immediately began to look for opportunities to work with church youth. Before we married, she was seeking a church that needed help with youth and had volunteered to be a Girl Scout leader for a blind troop. I have also noticed that teenagers easily adapt to her.

There is vigorous participation among the youth in the Walther League. Mr. and Mrs. Pope Huff are dedicated enthusiastic Christlike leaders for the group. Youth members are encouraged to bring nonmember friends, especially friends who are unchurched. I have noticed at least 50 youth in attendance on a Friday night with no bad-behavior incidents. I work closely with the youth devotional leaders and purposely have personal fun chats with as many teenagers as I can on any meeting night.

On Pentecost 1962 our class of 14 youth is confirmed. Immediately following the service, one of the Women's Auxiliary leaders, Mary Harris, approaches Jean and pleads with her to start a youth choir with the new group. I use the term *plead* because Jean tells me that she declines at first and recommends some of the public-school music teachers in the church. Then Mrs. Harris explains that music professionals had taken over other confirmation classes to have a choir but each group disintegrated within a few months. She says she wants to see this group stay together and be active in church and that Jean is the only person she knows who can do the job. When Mrs. Harris promises to help with the group, Jean accepts and supervises it weekly. Other youth join, and one is an excellent pianist; they use two-part music, with an older teenager as director, and sing every second Sunday as Jean continues the very necessary supervision. Noteworthy to me is that it is an all-girl choir. Even though boys refuse to join, they appear on the two front pews in church on the Sundays when the choir sings.

December 1962. A son, Roger, is born on a Walther League meeting night, and I call the church as they requested. They already know that Jean has been in the hospital all of that day.

Jean's mother comes to stay and help for a few weeks. We realize the great need after she has been with us for a few days. Jean and I had no additional persons to help us when Jocelyn and Jann were born.

When Roger is about seven weeks old, Jean begins placing him on a blanket on the floor so that the sisters can enjoy him easier than reaching through his crib. His vigorous activity and floor exercises surprise us.

Ten of our Walther Leaguers accompany me to the Northern Illinois Walther League convention. We were the only African Americans in attendance with 600 Walther Leaguers, their pastors, and adult leaders. During the convention, I am elected Northern Illinois District pastoral advisor. Following the election results, two strong boys lift me on their shoulders and proceed to the stage while the group rallies a favorite show-off of squeals, clapping hands, and stomping their feet.

The Walther League position causes me to travel to cities and towns in Illinois, Indiana, and Wisconsin. In Rockford, Ill., I am addressing 300 or more youth in a park on oneness in Christ and include some of the difficulties experienced in growing up and as a pastor. As I speak, a pastor in the rear of the gathering yells, "We don't want to hear that kind of stuff; we don't want to hear it. If that is what you want to talk about, you can go home." I stop and say, "Walther Leaguers, what should I do?" A youth officer stands and speaks, "He is not speaking on our behalf. We invited you. Please continue." A deafening applause with squeals erupts. As I am about to continue, another pastor stands and states that the pastor in the rear has spoken neither on behalf of the youth nor the other pastors in attendance. In a few days I receive a call from the outspoken pastor. He apologizes and asks my forgiveness. I accept the apology and state my forgiveness, but decline the invitation he extends to preach at his church.

A Story of two Graduate Schools

After doing well in my courses, one each of two semesters at the University of Chicago, I decide that I would like to pursue a doctoral degree in theology at Garrett Theological Seminary in Evanston. I ask three persons to write letters of recommendation as required by the director of graduate studies. One of the persons asked is my circuit counselor who said he would gladly write on my behalf. Upon receiving a letter from the graduate school informing me that I was declined admission, I immediately go to see the director of graduate studies who explains that it is not he who caused the refusal. "I must tell you exactly what happened. Your circuit counselor stated in his letter that he is not recommending you. We cannot accept you."

Soon as possible, I talk with my circuit counselor. I ask, "Why would you decline to recommend me after giving me your promise?" He replies, "Robert, you are doing a marvelous job at St. Philip's Church and many people on Chicago's south side have been blessed through your work." I respond, "I have some dreams and ambitions in mind for my work in the church beyond the local level inclusive of remaining a pastor." As I leave the pastor's office, I begin to recall that there might be more to my rejection than appears. Two of Garrett's chief administrators have persistently and consistently asked me to leave the Lutheran church, become Methodist, and receive scholarships and part-time work in Chicago churches. I have repeatedly declined. Nonetheless, I had completed 22 credits with excellent grades at Garrett before the rejection calamity.

I enroll in the Lutheran School of Theology in Chicago. The experiences in the New Testament course remain of great interest. The course is centered around the synoptic gospels. Dr. Voobis insists on the students reading and translating the Greek New Testament orally. I am recalling that whenever a student declined, Dr. Voobis would say, "Mr. King." I was one of the best performers in the class for reading and translating Greek. Also, I was the only African American. Now I am thinking of the theologian and scholar, Dr. Nau, who taught my Greek courses at Immanuel. I am also reflecting on my graduation from a nonaccredited seminary and thanking God that all past years' learning is helpful to me now. I am also thinking that through strategic planning, Immanuel could have become an accredited seminary. My alma mater was closed.

Jean shares my feelings of loss whenever I talk with her about the closing. Also, Jocelyn likes to join in by telling us that she did not want my school to close. She has only seen it once. I have talked with pastors Foard and Griffen who are Immanuel graduates with churches in Chicago. We can only share our common feelings of regret. The topic of closing has been discussed by synodical and district officials for three or more years. I mailed my input, prayed, and hoped. The week that I received the unpleasant news, my family knew that I was hurtfully disappointed. I have learned that similar concern has been raised about our school in Selma.

Europe

During the summer of 1963 I become a member of a tour group led by Dr. Andrew Schulze and Dr. Ralph Moellering. Our primary destination is the Lutheran World Federation Assembly in Helsinki, Finland. St. Philip's Church approves and is supportive of this five-week tour. I am able to develop a valuable slide collection using the new camera purchased for the trip. Our tour reaches 11 European countries, including Russia.

In Red Square we visit the mausoleum where Lenin's body lies in state, guarded by soldiers. Hundreds of people are in line daily to view his body. With Communism in control in Moscow and Leningrad, many of the Christian churches and cathedrals are closed and some of them surrounded with iron fences and locked gates. Elderly women are seen going up to the cathedrals, genuflecting and making the sign of the cross. On weekends, young children are taken out of the city to special camps to learn Communism. It is disheartening seeing church buildings being used for museums, or empty.

There are Lutheran churches in Germany and many Roman Catholic churches. Only a few people attend any of the churches. The same is true in the Scandinavian countries, which are mostly Lutheran. We are told that many Scandinavians attend church four times while on earth—Baptism, confirmation, marriage, and death. As I begin my trip home, I am certain that I would not like to go to Europe again and stay five weeks. I feel that the tour was too long for me and my purposes. I was often realizing that Jean was alone with the three children and all of the other responsibilities.

Lasting Memories

While I am at St. Philip's Church, the venerable Dr. Carter is taken to glory after approximately 50 years in the holy ministry. While ministering to him in the hospital near death, I ask him to bless me as Abraham blessed Isaac and as Isaac blessed Jacob. He agrees. As I kneel by his bed, he pronounces a blessing, laying his hand upon me and speaking words I shall never forget. I know that God does the blessing. The blessing God gave me through Dr. Carter continues with me.

Reflecting on my years with Dr. Carter, it appears that both of us encountered blessed early experiences. Also, I feel like a son of Dr. Carter as I recall the numerous times he shared one or more of the incidents that occurred in his early work. On one occasion in his living room, I ask him to give the sequenced details about his ministry in Chicago. My question elicits a radiant smile from him. With enthusiasm and seriousness, he begins telling how he began St. Philip's in the YMCA on Wabash Street by gathering a few people and conducting worship services in 1924:

I left the mission field in Alabama that was started by Rosa Young and was stationed here by the Missionary Board to lecture in the Midwestern churches to raise funds for the mission work in Alabama. Of course, to be effective, I learned German. Nearly everywhere I went, Lutherans seemed to have responded positively and genuinely.

After getting tired of traveling and preaching in German all over the Midwest, I considered it timely to have a congregation of my own. I was led hopefully by the Holy Spirit to start St. Philip's at a place available—the YMCA.

The little congregation worshiped there until we acquired a two-story building at Sixty-fourth and St. Lawrence. I established my residence on the second floor and developed a chapel for worship on the first floor.

I recall the building had coal heat and two or more tons of coal were usually deposited between the street and the building. I used a wheelbarrow to transport the coal and dump it into the basement coal den.

Gee! That was hard manual labor! But the Lord blessed the congregation and we were able to get help eventually. We became the first Negro congregation, as far as I know, to become self-sup-

porting. We stayed in the two-story building
until we bought the church at 6232 Eberhart.

I bought the parsonage across the street. I am
happy for you and your family, Bishop, that you
should have an easier and more enjoyable parish
experience than my family and I had during the
early days of St. Philip's.

It is all by the grace, mercy, and goodness of
God. May He bless you and your family as you
continue the work of our Savior's saving kingdom.

When Dr. Carter finishes, I am silent for a few seconds.
I can only say, "I thank God that you were sent." His dis-
course has startled me, and as I leave, the words have indeli-
bly imprinted my memory.

Six months after officiating Dr. Carter's funeral, his
son, attorney Marmaduke Carter Jr., dies. According to his
written instructions, he is buried in an unpainted pine box
with his body wrapped in a sheet. He had also requested that
any money that would have been needed for funeral furnishings should be used to buy clothing and food for poor children on Forty-seventh Street.

A Different Dwelling Appears

March 1965. We learn that our members, William and
Minnie Rutledge are selling a nearly new brick bungalow
four blocks from the church. We have already begun to look
for more space for our family of five, preferably a single-fam-
ily home. The Rutledges gladly permit us to arrange for the
purchase. When the house was built, Mr. Rutledge, a car-
penter, did most of the work. Their lawn is thick and well cul-
tivated. They have built a large, covered veranda in the back-

yard for their outdoor living and entertaining. This home's interior is spacious and beautiful. As we consider our two-year old, Roger, their chain-link fence is very important.

We move in April. On our first morning in the new home, I open the door and tell Roger it is all right to go out. All of us go to a window to watch him meet his first fence. We don't see him at first so we try another window. Roger is placing his foot into the last link at the top—ready to go or fall to the sidewalk.

Our new location is excellent for Jocelyn's bike-riding, and Jann is starting to ride the two-wheeler given her by the Griffens.

Final Days at St. Philip's

While reading notices on a bulletin board at the Lutheran School of Theology of Chicago, I observe that Indiana University is offering three Lilly Fellowships in adult education. I apply and send all required documents. Jean and I pray fervently. A few weeks pass. We wait. A letter arrives from Indiana University. I did not open it at once. I take this letter to the church, lay it before the altar, pray to God and ask that He give me an answer concerning my return to school, primarily to pursue a doctoral degree. I pray to God that if it is not His will, the answer is no; if it is His will, the answer is yes. After finding consolation to cease praying, I open the envelope. The letter reads, "It is the pleasure of Indiana University to grant you a Lilly Fellowship effective September 1965." That is only two months away.

Within the next two weeks I consult with my district president, who gives his approval and blessings. I am also wished God-speed by the president and academic dean of Concordia Teachers College, River Forest.

The most difficult distance to travel now is my time period between July and September. It is beginning to burden me. Suddenly, low, sad hours are frequently occurring. I pray diligently for God's strength to help me to leave His St. Philip's, not mine. The adjoining building to be constructed is God's, not mine. The elegant architect's design is displayed in the front entry of the church.

For the past three years, the members and I have worked towards finalizing plans for renovation and an adjoining multipurpose building. Plans include a daycare center with kindergarten potential and an outdoor sports facility erected on the top of the new structure. God is very worthy to be praised as I see and hear the members' interest in children and youth demonstrated in their building plans. This overt focus on the young is remarkable growth during my nearly eight years as pastor.

Leaving means that I shall not be seeing St. Philip's through the building program. I need God's power to leave and accept a blessing that I requested in prayer. As days come and go, I am feeling that God is specifically guiding me to begin increasing the range and scope of my ministry while keeping my promise that I will go and preach.

I have seen a sample of the Christmas cards showing the architect's design. Perhaps I will be able to obtain one of them.

My letter to St. Philip's tenders my resignation effective the first week of September. Both Jean and Jocelyn are frequently assuring me that they really want me to pursue this academic venture. Jann, five years old, perhaps does not quite understand, and has said, "That's all right." Roger, age 2, will probably give me his retroactive approval when he is older.

We are glad that a more convenient family home has been obtained for our arrangements at this time. When we secured the house, we had no idea that I would be leaving St. Philip's.

I plan to return from Indiana University each Friday

night and stay until Sunday afternoon. We are believing that family plans are adequate as possible. We have a kind woman for child care. Jean is continuing in the position she requested, teaching child development and family living in a public high school reserved for pregnant teens only. She has learned to drive very well after rushing to get her driver's license just before I went to Europe in 1963. I am sure that I'm leaving our car in excellent condition. A used Renault is being purchased for my travel.

It is my hope that as soon as possible, within a school term, we can all be together in Indiana, provided adequate housing and professional employment for Jean are available. However, my unannounced detail is that if this is not possible, I will transfer the Indiana University credits to one of the universities in or near Chicago and continue along with a part-time job. Certainly God will guide us through this undertaking.

8

Indiana University

The Departure

Sunday, Sept. 11, 1965. I am leaving tonight but talking with Jean about the hacking cough Jocelyn has today. Jean reminded me of Dr. Wirtshafter's advice.

"When his prescription doesn't work, let him see her."

"When can you take her?"

"I plan to take a day off tomorrow."

"Good, maybe he'll change the prescription again."

Jocelyn, age 11, is a healthy child with the exception of sometimes having asthmatic bronchitis. But the attacks have seldom appeared during the past two years. Jocelyn is reminding me to take a bag of the cookies she baked yesterday.

The next day, Monday afternoon, I call home. Jean explains that Jocelyn has pneumonia but it is mild in one lung and she must stay out of school for the week, then return to the doctor to be certain she is back to normal.

The Vigil for Jocelyn

On Tuesday, about noon, Jean calls me at Indiana

University to say that Jocelyn is in the Bob Roberts Children's Hospital of the University of Chicago Medical Center. Immediately, I take a plane to Chicago and a taxi to the hospital. Jocelyn is lying in a coma in the ICU. The doctor had worked with Jean by telephone for part of the preceding night. Early this morning, he came to the house and called an ambulance. A particle from a lung dislodged while Jocelyn was coughing, traveled through the blood stream, and burst a vessel in the left brain, forming a clot.

When I arrive, Jean has just left to go home for a few minutes. I stand and stare at Jocelyn's motionless body; I pray. Finally, I call her name and her entire body jerks. Then her body flinches hard each time I call her. But I stop because it seems she might damage one of the three instruments attached to her. One of her jerks was extremely vigorous. In a few moments the door opens wide and the bed ordered for Jean is brought into the room. The doctor has given Jean permission to stay in Jocelyn's room.

Soon, Jean is back. She tells me that when she called our friend, Pastor William Griffen, he came to the hospital shortly after Jocelyn was admitted and prayed. He stayed with Jean until she had contacted me.

Jean lets me know that Mrs. Eldora Hayes, a member of our church who takes care of the children, has voluntarily taken Jann and Roger to her home. Moreover, Jean has loaned her a key for entrance to our home. Now we just stand there, looking at Jocelyn. We sit and talk before I go home and leave Jean in the room where she will sleep tonight.

As Jocelyn lay in a coma the third day, Dr. Wirtshafter, her pediatrician, is continuously saying that she has puzzled all of the doctors. He has alerted many pediatricians in Chicago to see Jocelyn and to advise if they can. Dr. Wirtshafter has also informed us that a search reveals that only two children in Chicago are in the records for Jocelyn's condition. Neither of them lived over 24 hours. Our daughter has pneumonia and a stroke.

On the fourth day, Dr. Wirtshafter reports that he has just reprimanded two of the hospital's physicians. He learned that they told us Jocelyn would not likely live and that we should proceed with appropriate plans and they did not consult him. He is very angry with the doctors. He tells us, "Just watch her and see. I told those doctors to shut up. I know the health Jocelyn had, and I believe she will make it." Jean and I leave; go home; shed a few tears together; pray; laugh; thank God for all of His mercies; and go to Mrs. Hayes' home to visit Jann and Roger.

Saturday, day 5, my three sisters arrive from Detroit. Jean's mother has called and is coming tomorrow. Today, I call every pastor I know and request prayers for tomorrow's Sunday worship services.

Monday is day 7. After a Sunday night of doctors and nurses rushing in and out of the room with more zest than any night, the hospital's chief pediatrician tells me personally to come with him to a small office. He says, "I'm sure you are wondering why we have been in such a frenzy, rushing around last night and this morning."

"Yes," I replied. "We thought there was something you did not want to tell us, that is, perhaps she is dying."

He answered, "We have good news, but we have been busy checking her to be absolutely sure. Due to supernatural providence and with no help from us, the clot disintegrated last night, and she is now only sleeping. Your daughter is no longer in a coma."

Jean and I thank God for bringing Jocelyn through. With total right side paralysis, her speech has to return slowly and a wheel chair must be used until sufficient mobility returns to her right side.

A number of caring people made an indelible impression upon us. While Jocelyn was in the coma, an elder from St. Philip's came in a taxi to our home, left it waiting, rushed in to tell us that she will be all right and left. Another elder also came in a rush to tell us the same and said to be sure to pray. I told him I was praying. He then added, "You must get on your knees until they are 'gritty,' ask the Lord to have pity and she will be healed." An older lady who lived in front of the church, came, brought by her daughter, looked skyward and said she had received a message that our daughter will be healed. She added that she prays at the same time three times daily, morning, noon, and evening.

When Jean's mother prepares to leave us, she insists that she take Roger, our two-year-old with her. She said, "In this way I can lighten your responsibilities for when Jocelyn comes home." Roger was delighted to talk about going on the bus with Grandma.

After three weeks, Jocelyn is released from the hospital. Dr. Wirtshafter advises me to return to school because Jocelyn is safely recuperating and tells me that I can do no more than offer companionship. Jean has obtained an emergency leave of absence. Upon the doctor's suggestion and judgment, I return to the university and will certainly be back on Fridays, sometimes Thursdays.

A Prayer Meeting and Strangely, More

As I come back and forth, home and to school, friends are continuing to contact us as they check on Jocelyn. Later in the fall we learn that when St. Philip's members heard about Jocelyn's illness and on that same Sunday morning of the night that the clot began to disintegrate, they held an "old-fashioned" prayer meeting for her after the worship service. We are told that there were many prayers and tears. According to an elder, the official vacancy pastor waits for the prayers to end so that he can participate in the voters' meeting scheduled. He continues to explain that this pastor was unaware that several men had organized a schism to occur during the meeting. The group recruited members who usually did not attend to come help their cause during this special meeting. The schismaticals wanted a different vacancy pastor and new guidelines for procedures. But when the prayers for Jocelyn end, there are two strange occurrences: (1) a record number of men attend the meeting, (2) the would-be schism group remains silent; the meeting is peaceful and productive. He is explaining that prayers to God in unity for Jocelyn reunited the people. Then he simply concludes, "Your daughter's illness has saved that congregation from a split and division."

Probation?

It is December 1965. I have been returning home on weekends and now it is Christmas break. Jocelyn's recovery has been rapid, surprising her doctors and the hospital physicians. She is riding her bike again. Her return to the sixth-grade classroom is on Dec. 8, Jean's birthday, after seven weeks of out-patient physical therapy. By telephone and letters, we believe that Roger is having a wonderful time with his grandparents in Asheville. Jean, the girls, and I are making several holiday visits to friends' homes, especially those who monitored us so kindly when Jocelyn was ill. Jocelyn and Jann are making the presentations of the loaves of dessert breads Jean baked and gift-wrapped, one for each of those friends. Jann has been looking forward to going bowling again. So we do, just the two of us.

My grades arrive and a letter is enclosed informing me that I am on probation. The three weeks out of school when Jocelyn was ill seem to have had some effect. My grade point average is 3.2. There is a recently established policy in the school of education. In all of the other schools for various fields of study, students in the doctoral programs must maintain a GPA of 3.00 or better. But students pursuing a Ph.D. in education are now required to hold at least a 3.5. I must pray, work, and wait.

At home after the second semester ends, the mail carrier brings the expected envelope. I am wondering if I am off probation. I rip the envelope and see five A's, a 4.00 GPA for my second semester. Praise the Lord!

Indiana Kindness to Our Rescue

I am eligible to continue but I have family concerns too. I have told a fellow Lutheran, Dick Pell, a professor at the university, about my desire to have the family together. Through him, I am interviewed by an assistant superintendent of schools on Jean's behalf. Next, this superintendent interviews Jean and offers her a position in special education for secondary school students. But there is a waiting list for university housing for families. During the same week that Jean is given employment, we are miraculously permitted to sign a lease to live in Tulip Tree House, the most recent construction for students with families. We shall live in a large five-room apartment with two full baths on the seventh floor of the 11-story building. Five acres of well-equipped playground are surrounded with chain-link fence much taller than ours in Chicago that failed the Roger Test. The top rows of barbed wire do not give this fence much appeal. Nonetheless we do not plan to allow him out alone. He returned from the grandparents in May. With arrangements finalized in Indiana, our big job of moving is next.

Preparation to leave Chicago includes a surprise emergency for Jann. Her school has sent a note stating that she did not pass the vision test given to all students. The note comes as Jann is completing her kindergarten year, and it instructs us to have her checked by an eye specialist. Jean does not do this immediately and has said that she will certainly take care of it soon. Finally, they go to a specialist but are told that Jann's eyes needed a correction available through only one doctor on Chicago's south area. We learn that there is a waiting list for his service. We are surprised at Jann's need because she loves reading stories, is an excellent reader, and had been sent into a second grade room for reading, daily, since her second month in kindergarten. Finally, the specialist can see Jann late in the summer, and we learn that even though she read books, her sight is limited to only several feet.

Late August 1966. We rent our house to a friend and leave for Tulip Tree House on Indiana University's campus. Jocelyn, in grade 7, and Jann, first grade, will enroll in University School across the highway by our apartment building. Roger will attend the day-care center.

In our apartment, Jean likes to talk about some of the child-safe features as she discovers them. Because of Roger, the explorer, we especially like the hidden wall box that allows a person to deactivate any single electrical receptacle in any room. Even the range and disposal are easily turned off from this box.

There is a special safety concern for Jean and the children, generally. Before leaving Chicago, she said that strange boys were beginning to romp through our neighborhood and disappear. Two friends had received serious head injuries while walking only one block from our house, and the assailants fled each time. Our next-door neighbor told Jean that the sidewalks are high risk because gangs are sending members into the neighborhood in twos to commit crimes and run. Whenever Jean left the house in the evening, she sent for an adult to stay with the children. In Tulip Tree House, and only after a few days here, Jocelyn is asking to accept a baby-sitting job upstairs, and if she does, gang members will not be a concern.

Soon after arriving, my kind friend who obtained a teaching position for Jean and helped us to be able to come to Indiana invites all of us to his home, where we meet his lovely wife, Dorothy, and son. A few weeks later he is instantly killed by a drunk driver when returning from teaching a class at the university's other campus. This hurts Jean and me. As soon as we heard the news she said, "God used him to bring us here." I certainly agree with her. Personally, I am very sad about it. Before my family came, he and I had several conversations. I found him to be a very Christlike person. He was superintendent of the Faith Lutheran Sunday School.

Early School News

February 1967. All of my Lilly Foundation Fellowship funds are used. But I have a graduate assistant position in the department of education which I am able to handle even with my full course load. Studies are no easier than last year. I am trying to complete the adult-education doctoral requirements, inclusive of electives in educational psychology. Towards the total requirement, each of my 22 Garrett Theological Seminary credits have been applied. When members of my committee discussed transfer credits with me, the chairperson and two others complimented Garrett on being one of the best in the United States. The committee accepted ten semester hours from the University of Pittsburgh, where I earned a master of education degree. They provided written acknowledgment that I had earned a master's degree even though most of the credits applied were from Garrett. With this positive news in mind, I am more certain of how much lies ahead to be accomplished. This semester demands serious study for comprehensive exams while doing my internship at the Indiana Women's Prison and continuing working for the education department.

Jocelyn and Jann are enjoying University School. They are in their second semester and no problems in studying or adaptation have surfaced. Certainly we have had a few quiet concerns regarding Jocelyn, but her actions appear to be congruent with Dr. Wirtshafter's opinion in August of last year, "Complete recovery." She recently showed us her bull's-eye score sheets from rifle practice in the physical-education class. She is delighted because classmates who laughed at her clumsiness in the basketball and volleyball classes are unable to score as she does in the rifle unit. Jann is still an exceptional reader. This school's practice is to have four first grade classrooms according to reading ability. She remains in the top group and is one of the four selected to sit-in for the fourth grade science sessions. I have visited the school only a few times and met the teachers. Jean has been able to be involved whenever requests are made for parents to be present.

Jean "Stands through My Exam"

Students often talk about their fear and anxiety for the doctoral comprehensive examinations. I am no exception. It is mid-spring 1967, and my family knows that I am approaching a crisis point. I am in more intensive study than my first year because it is crucial for me to pass all sections of the exams. Failure in one of the sections will delay the date that I am permitted to begin my dissertation. Recently, I have listened to students who suffered delays because of failing part of the "comps." On a Monday morning the first day has arrived, and according to instructions, I must allow three days for all of the writing followed by the orals on a near future date. This same morning, Jean awakens with a spasm-type pain in her neck and shoulder and cannot move her head. She calls her school and takes a day off, and the pain is nearly gone by evening. She later explained that during the night before my first day's exam, she had an extremely clear dream of an exam room in which several men were writing and a wife standing by each, holding and handing papers to the husband. The only words she remembered hearing were mine telling her, "This year our wives are permitted to come to the exam room and help us." She said that this dream with all appropriate colors was vivid and very real. She stood, holding papers for me and looking down at my desk with her head tilted to her left side. The next morning she felt as if she had stood for hours, and her head was actually fastened toward her left shoulder, and she could not turn it without pain. She says I was smiling during the exam. The room, proctor, windows, and all are still mysteriously clear to her. My orals are taken the following week. The exam results were excellent. The questions were not nearly as difficult as I had imagined. A great hurdle is over, and I can proceed with completion of the foreign-language requirements. Thankfully, the Danish required for the adult education major was not difficult for me. However, some of the students applied much effort to survive. I was granted permission to add more Danish courses beyond the adult-education requirements and apply the work as one of my minors. A second-foreign language is still needed. I plan to enroll in the German course that generates eight credits in seven weeks this summer.

A German Summer

The German class begins. It meets four hours in the morning and four hours in the afternoon with two professors, one for each half-day session. My earlier German at Immanuel is very supportive. I am spending more time with the family and taking the children out for fun some evenings. Sometimes I cook dinner and Jean is surprised. Inasmuch as my course does not appear to be strenuous, I have persuaded Jean to take a summer graduate course. She had added a few in Chicago. Jean reluctantly listens to me and enrolls. She has been insisting that there will be no return to any graduate study for her until I finish.

On a Monday morning, the afternoon of my fourth week, the professors begin with three new books furnished as part of the high price of the course. The professors bring the books to class and I am seeing the pages for the first time. Suddenly I am lost! The three semesters of German at Immanuel were covered by these professors during the past three weeks. All of this is new. In this large class for doctoral students only, I notice that I am not the only student in trouble, perhaps frightened. After class many of us are buzzing about study groups. I elect to study with two men who seem to share my dilemma. We meet four hours during noon and evening. As the days pass, I am surviving well but the children see me only during dinner. I am with my study group until about 9:30 P.M. All of this is overwhelming. I held a 3.9 plus average in 18 credits of Danish with no help. Danish is a Germanic language, but this is the real German I am studying. Days are still bright and sunny after dinner and Jean is telling me that the children take turns saying, "Where is Daddy?" They are continuously asking if I am going to take them off campus anymore. We have a person to watch the children while Jean is in her one-evening-weekly class, but she has the other responsibilities that I had planned to assume. I really regret this predicament.

As the seven weeks end, I think I have a wonderful idea. I tell Jean, "Select any of the August two-week seminars you wish, enroll, and I will take the children to Alabama with me to visit Papa and his family. You will have no other responsibilities." She exclaims, "I'll love it!" Our departure date is near and Jean gladly packs for all of us. The evening before the morning that we are leaving, Jann suddenly gets a stomach infection. Our doctor forbids her to travel.

At the end of the two weeks, when I return with Jocelyn and Roger, Jean boasts of how surprisingly well everything turned out, including her three-credit course. But she adds that a very odd and unusual statement was made by Jann a few minutes after we left. Jean noticed that Jann was sitting very still, just staring. Jean said that she walked toward her and Jann held up her head and said, "Mommy, I'll be good." Of course Jean gave her a big hug. Perhaps the trip was a special experience. Jann seemed to be quite grown-up for those two weeks. A very nice person looked after her, and there was even some time for a few mother-and-daughter outings.

Father's Blessing

While talking to Jean about the trip, I revealed a wonderful experience I had with Papa while we were alone and he was ill, lying in bed. I did not know the weakening effects of his illness until we arrived—cancer. My father pronounces a blessing on me from his bed, asking God to bless me, be kind and gracious to me, and let me have a successful and productive life in the holy ministry. I am certain Papa's blessing will stay with me.

Alice

This summer I disclosed to Jean a commitment I voluntarily made with her mother. When Mama McCord and I were having a very pleasant conversation alone, she mentioned Jean's earlier graduate work and said that she had certainly hoped she would complete her master's degree someday. I was really glad to hear her and immediately replied, "Mama, I want you to know now that I will see that she completes the degree." Jean's sister, Ruth, had already finished hers during summers at New York University. It seems that I finally had to disclose that conversation to Jean.

Fall 1967. I am with the children one evening weekly while Jean takes a class. Both of us are aware that next semester my work will be more intense. We have decided that we should try to find a student who will share Jocelyn's room and be available to help with Roger and Jann. Our ad in the campus paper only brings one response, Alice Phang from Taiwan who had nearly completed her master's degree in piano. Alice accepts and is great for the children. She likes to share her Chinese cooking with them. They brag about the Chinese food. Jocelyn and Jann enjoy hanging around her, but she is learning that Roger frequently prefers being out of sight, which is sometimes a positive but often a negative. While this building is very child-safe, he can find strange ways to use some of our household items. Enough said. This book is not intended to tattle on Roger. Alice tells us the children in Taiwan are easier to watch than Roger. But she and Roger are good friends. She is already asking if he can be a ring bearer for her wedding. All of her relatives are in Taiwan.

Also during the fall of 1967, my second internship is at the Muscattutuck Hospital and Training Center, where I work with retarded adults. I am there two week days and some evenings. This book does not include details on practical training in planning and implementing educational programs for professionals who desire training. Those events are the Indiana Institutes conducted by a professor while students observe and/or participate. On one occasion, I serve as the administrator. The six-step Indiana Plan is utilized. With my activities gradually increasing, appreciation for Alice is very apparent.

Papa's Farewell

In October, I receive a telephone call from my sister,

Carrie, in Detroit telling me that she understands Papa's condition has worsened and his illness is now critical. She tells me that the family feels that any person desiring to see him alive should go home at once. Because I had already visited him in Alabama with two of the children in August, my better judgment was to accept the information and wait. Within three days she calls again to tell me that Papa has passed from this life. I allow a necessary interruption in the Muscattutuck work and leave immediately. On the evening before the funeral, as we are assembling to go to the funeral home for the "wake," only one of his 16 children is absent. Henry is to come from Germany. We are very thankful to see him walk into the house just as we are leaving. The next morning Papa's funeral is held at Shady Grove Baptist Church in Sunny South, Ala., where he had served as a deacon for many years. He is buried alongside his wife, my Mama Della.

Later at home a very important picture is taken. It shows all of his children—the first time ever that all of us are home at the same time. This funeral has much meaning for me, for I know that Papa's blessing is with me and he is with God. I am remembering his blessing.

Rejection Comes and Goes

Late November 1967. I complete the research course that clutches the initial writing for the dissertation. It is imperative that I present the first three chapters of my dissertation proposal as early in January as possible. Our good friends upstairs, Fred and Rita Barsun, are inviting me to work on my proposal in their apartment during the three weeks they will be gone for the holidays. They seem to enjoy monitoring my progress and have also kept a kind and loving watch over our family consistently. Fred is an elder in the University Lutheran Church.

I litter their kitchen table with my typewriter, books,

papers, and more papers stacked on the floor and chairs. I am carefully developing the precise plan agreed upon by both my committee chairman and the research professor. I thank God that all of my coursework is completed so that study time from now on can be committed to writing my dissertation. I work and rework through the information. Finally, as the Barsuns return I am able to submit my package to a dissertation typist who also lives here in Tulip Tree House.

After a few days of back and forth corrections with the typist, I prepare four copies, one for each of my doctorate committee members and present them to my chairman in his office. He will set a date with the others to meet with me. I leave feeling very confident that the proposal is adequately prepared and believing it will be accepted.

Two weeks later I am sitting with the committee of three, answering questions and explaining my procedures. One member, my Danish professor, is absent. The representative from the School of Education is not prepared to accept one of the limitations of the proposal but in this case, my chairman immediately provides justification. This is not surprising inasmuch as the chairman had previously guided me to do exactly as presented. But all is not well. One of the three professors gives me a rough time and appears to show furor for some sections of the proposal. I am surprised because I know the professor very well. This behavior is unlike him and actually appears superficial. I am excused as is the custom and wait outside. My confidence is weakening. Finally I am asked to return and the chairman states, "Mr. King, the committee has discussed your proposal and has decided to decline it."

I am sick. Dr. Blaisdell, the committee member who was absent sends for me to give his apology for his absence and then asks, "How was everything?" I answer, "The proposal was declined." "What?" he questions excitedly. "I read my copy of your proposal very carefully. Also, I have read many proposals in that department. Yours was one of the best, and that is why I did not think I would need to be at the meeting." This professor seems almost as upset as I am. He continues, "Set a date for another meeting. I will be there. In the meanwhile, read all you can and be prepared for most any question. Your study addresses older adults. Therefore be sure you are very familiar with characteristics, traits, and all pertinent information and again, I assure you, I will be there." Then he comes from behind his desk. "If they decline your proposal again, they need not send anymore students for Danish to this Germanic department. I will not be cooperative at all."

As I am leaving, it is almost amusing to consider his last statement because he is the only Danish instructor, and all students specializing in adult education are required to take at least six credits in this language.

I did not request an early date for another committee meeting. I strengthened my knowledge in the areas addressed in the proposal and considered alternatives if by any unforeseen action I have to delay my degree. During this time I consider two full-time employment offers. One is to become the campus pastor of University Lutheran Church and the other is minister of education for St. Peter Lutheran Church, Columbus, Ind., a congregation with over two thousand members. I am declining both because I think I should avoid full-time employment on campus or elsewhere until the completion of my dissertation. At best, I am sure that full-time appointments should be avoided until this proposal phase is safely ended and the actual further writing is progressing. Finally, during my weeks of waiting and pondering, I request an evaluation of my credits by the Graduate School for a master's degree in adult education while continuing towards the Ph.D. I receive an affirmative response and an invitation to the forthcoming convocation to receive a certificate for high scholastic achievement. This was not my matriculation focus but it was a welcome, grand feeling.

Four months have passed since my proposal was declined. The date I accept for the committee to meet again with me has come. The professor from the Germanic department is among the four. Again, I am given an oral exam on the proposal. At the end of the questioning period, the chairman and two of the members ask the professor who declined it previously if he has any questions. He responds, "I have no questions." This time the proposal is accepted. I am proceeding full speed ahead to finish my dissertation. Its most difficult hurdle is over and the ensuing writing should flow. The finalized title is the "Identification of Educational Needs of Older Adults in Three Congregate Facilities: A Diagnostic Study."

As I thank God for all good results so far, I also give thanks that during all of my busy activities, Jocelyn has been successfully participating in her confirmation class. In April 1968 she is confirmed at Faith Lutheran Church in Bloomington. University Lutheran Church did not have a youth confirmation class. University Church's focus is the college student and any faculty member who desires to attend. Later in April, we go to Alice's final piano recital. She will receive her master's degree in May. A few friends are helping her in preparation for her wedding in May, and Roger will be the ring bearer.

9

Concordia Teachers College, River Forest

Affirming Full-time Teaching Ministry

Early in 1968, I receive a letter inviting me to come to Concordia Teachers College, River Forest, Ill., for an informal conference to discuss my training, skills, and abilities in the areas of Christian adult education and general education. I accept the invitation.

The discussions are conducted by the president, academic dean, chairman of the graduate school and department of education and psychology. Soon after returning to Bloomington I receive a letter of appointment to the faculty of Concordia Teachers College as assistant professor of education and psychology, beginning July 1, 1968.

The offer is given prayers asking God's help for guidance. After two weeks, I write Concordia College a letter accepting the position. Certainly this means that we start packing, but preparation for moving includes other concerns inherent with our departure. Jean must inform her school officials that she is not returning this fall. We are discontinuing Jann's piano lessons, but in turn her teacher calls us. She states that she received our notice and needs to ask us to please continue Jann's lessons when we move. Then she reiterates her specialty that she only teaches beginners and that Jann was the fastest beginner she had taught during her ten teaching years. Jean needs to complete a two-week seminar early in June. I must arrange for my final internship, which is at St. Benedict College. I will decline participation in the commencement convocation. I was invited only because the degree is nearly completed, really meaning I passed the comprehensive exams. We must make arrangements for both moving and storing our furniture. This is because Steve Schmidt, a member of the Concordia faculty, and his wife are asking us to store our furniture and live in their home in Maywood near Concordia College for one year while their family is in New York, where Steve will complete work for his doctorate. We accept their offer. Now we shall have a year to get acquainted with our new location before deciding whether to buy a home or accept a faculty house.

Steve's offer includes very interesting information. He states that because African Americans have never lived in this corner of Maywood, he has gone door to door in each of the four blocks, surrounding his property and announced that he would be renting his home to an African American clergyman/professor and his family. He told us that many persons expressed acceptance, but some others protested, and a few slammed their doors. Steve said that he announced his intentions because of his belief that if the protesters were given a chance to scream at him and express opposition, they would not likely indulge in more protest behavior after we arrive.

The move to Maywood occurs at the end of June. We are entrusted all of the Schmidts' furniture, including their baby grand piano. This is a well-preserved two-story home where we are living on a busy street, Fifth Avenue. During our first few weeks, the pastor of St. Paul's Church in Melrose Park, several Lutheran community people and a friendly Italian family across the street seem to be taking turns in the afternoons standing in our yard or sitting on the porch, never hurrying to leave, and will not come inside. We heard of threats to damage the property but nothing has happened. Our children walk to St. Paul's School and to Walther High School. Jean is not applying for employment this fall semester. She wants to avoid working for a while and I agree. This is a rapid transition. She needs a break and we need her at home.

First-Year Activities Inclusive of a Goal Accomplished

Fall 1968. The courses I am teaching at Concordia College are religious instruction, educational psychology, youth leadership, and adult education. I am also giving any time I can spare towards completing my dissertation. It is a welcome relief to use the excellent typing service Concordia is providing for this purpose. A very appreciated responsibility is serving as advisor to the youth leadership program. Now I am extending the experiences I had with youth in Youngstown and the Northern Illinois District.

A few months after coming to Concordia, Fred Hampton, a gang member, is killed by lawmen in the Chicago area. Some of the African American students at Concordia attempt a small insurrection on the campus. Without any notification, someone posts a notice that there will be an African American student meeting with me in charge. On this same morning, I had promised to attend an important meeting in Chicago. As I leave the campus a faculty member stops me saying, "I was on my way over to hear you." I reply, "No one has asked, and I have not promised to serve as a consultant for this insurrection." I wondered why no communication from an administrator or students was sent to me.

On June 1, 1969, Jean and I are out of the house for a while in the afternoon. We return to find a room filled with guests shouting, "Happy Anniversary." Our friends, the Sievings and others, including President Martin Koehneke had schemed with Jocelyn to have a celebration for our 20th wedding anniversary. The surprise was festive with good food, gifts, and loads of laughter.

Summer 1969. Dr. J. A. O. Preus asks me to develop and teach two courses in my area for Concordia Theological Seminary, Springfield, Ill. The courses I design are (1) "Adult Education in the Parish" and (2) "Christian Education in a Contemporary Society." Concordia College has cooperatively permitted me to leave the academic year one week early to accommodate teaching the courses. During the first week of July, I leave Springfield for two days to travel to Indiana and defend my dissertation, which I believe is a God-blessed charge. The dissertation is defended successfully. The degree will be awarded the following Dec. 2, 1969, and I will decline participation in the Graduate School Convocation. Attending my commencement seems to have little to add to the great relief I feel. Perhaps, knowledge that I have a choice is sufficient. My prayers and thanks to God are even more sufficient. Again, the cherished words of Matthew 6:33 are apparent.

Our year in the Schmidts' house is ending, and we opt to accept faculty housing, a two-story eight-room home in Oak Park, about the same distance from the campus as the house in Maywood. The dwelling has basic features that make it very adequate and comfortable. The floors, walls, and everything are in good condition, kept up by the college. Our furniture is an excellent fit for the rooms. The one necessity is treatment for the windows, and Jean takes care of them with new drapes and curtains.

Same as in Maywood, we are in an all-white community. While we were moving, and during an interval between trips, our home was burglarized. Items stolen included a television, slide projector, and a portable sewing machine. The house was ransacked as if someone was also looking for money. The burglary seemed to be a first for this neighborhood.

Jocelyn and Jann appear to have made an excellent adaptation to their different school system of all Lutheran schools, and Roger has done remarkably well in kindergarten. Jann is continuing piano lessons and Jocelyn has begun piano again for the first time since her stroke. During grade 3, she had once won the Chicago parochial school piano competition. She was enrolled in St. Peter's Lutheran School.

Jann and Roger were not born when we took short summer trips to the rustic cabins in Canada. This summer all five of us travel to the north shore of Lake Erie, where we stay for a few days, continuing on to Detroit. We rent a large two-room cabin very close to the water near a fishing wharf, and I catch more fish than planned. The children have fun on the wharf and in the sand. The place is not conducive for swimming, and wading seems risky. We still have a wonderful time.

With the Ph.D. pursuit accomplished, I still reflect on how Matthew 6:33 has surfaced through my thoughts since Pastor Jenkins admonished me at Good Shepherd Lutheran School. Also, I am continuing in my ambition to hold on to my first love, the pulpit. Therefore, with much thankfulness to God, I am accepting preaching opportunities in the college chapel and once monthly at First Immanuel Church, where I have begun to serve as assistant pastor.

I am able to enjoy more involvement at home now than last year. We keep a few games for fun and Jocelyn has added "Probe" to the collection. All of us only recently learned the rules, but it is fun in a challenging sort of way. Because of events that involve her, we are also frequently at Walther High School. But some of her activities do not include us. She has friends with whom she goes shopping, or for visits, parties, and teenage activities generally. Jann has added the Brownie troop to her activities. Jean serves as chauffeur for both of the girls. She is teaching but is home and available before the children arrive from school. I work through late afternoons and some evenings. Faculty fun and informal entertainment seem to pass from home to home. We are looking forward to sponsoring a faculty evening at our house next year.

Our chief problem among the three children is that Roger's teacher, Miss Mensing, at Grace Lutheran School, River Forest, continues to report that he is very reluctant to write. He is required to do at least some beginning writing in her first-grade class. She provides us with ideas that may help, and we are trying. Miss Mensing has told us that he entered the school year comprehending fourth-grade reading books and only wanting to write his name. We are following her suggestions and trying.

For family out-of-the-house action, all of us enjoy going to Chicago, only a short distance from our home, to visit old friends. Some of them, especially the Griffens, have children near the age of Jocelyn. Chicago has many great centers of interest including the Aquarium, the Museum of History, and the Art Institute. Whenever we make visits to those sites, Jocelyn conducts the tours because she has been to all of the places with school groups and again with her friends.

Mid-spring 1970. My sisters and brothers in Detroit give a celebration honoring the completion of my doctorate.

I have many cousins and relatives in Detroit. Therefore, when my family and I arrive, there is a big, loving crowd for the occasion.

At Concordia College, the spring semester is gradually coming to a close, and it seems that my work has been a very blessed and productive experience as I perceive it. The same opinion appears to generate from faculty and students. Evaluations have been especially positive. Already I have received my summer school course assignment. I will teach one course, "Teaching Adults," and conduct a workshop.

"Strangeness" at Concordia

As the summer begins, I am approached by teachers from Triton College who seem upset as they tell me that they came to Concordia to register for the "Teaching Adults" class and were told the course is canceled. They want to know why. I inform them that I have not heard anything of the sort and that I am ready to conduct the course. I send them back to the registrar and they return to tell me that the course is no longer canceled. I also learned that the course was in reality canceled without any notification to me. No one in administration seemed to be clear about the incident. Also there were sufficient students registering for the course for it to be taught.

Early in the summer I receive a letter directing me to accept another duty instead of teaching for fall 1970. My assignment is to work under a professor who would designate responsibilities to observe schools in various places, and make general reports about teachers, and the like. I inquire about an assignment of faculty courses to teach, as in the past four semesters, but my inquiry is met each time with answers meaning there is no assurance, and/or that I might just wait and see. A sudden chill appears to be blowing from Concordia College onto me. I would like answers; there are none. However, I am reminded that I do have an assignment for the fall. This assignment is precisely the equivalent to the work given to a graduate student who serves under a professor as an assistant.

I have one thought that may be relevant. There is pressure signaling serious bias against the two recent curricular areas of study introduced at the college: (1) early childhood education and (2) Christian adult education. I was present one evening when a professor denounced both, giving his reasoning. "This school was established to train teachers to teach students. We don't need anything about little kids and adults." Maybe he has been influential. The young woman who was assisted by the college to earn her Ph.D. in early childhood education was severely inhibited recently, and in turn, left immediately for a position at a university in Arizona. My intuition causes me to believe that my position is gradually becoming history. I am still conducting a workshop and course on campus this summer as I promised.

My decision is to follow through with the new assignment but to simultaneously allow a letter indicating my field of study to be sent to a few selected institutions that have potential for using my skills. In doing this, I will remember that I now and always plan to remain a minister, and it seems that I am a natural fit for the teaching ministry, same as some of my colleagues. Now I am looking forward to leaving Concordia College after another year, and I feel pushed by the college to leave if the professional training I have been using is ever to be used again.

Surprisingly, I receive offers to come and work this year at Valparaiso, Florida A & M, Claflin, and Lincoln University. Actually, I accepted the interview at Lincoln University of Missouri reluctantly, and I was thinking of next year, not this fall. The desire of the president to have me establish the first adult-education program in the central area of the state was very appealing. If I would accept, he is offering the rank of full professor, graduate courses, and an undergrad course all in the department of education, where I would develop the adult-education thrust. But I am also aware that I would be at a public institution, and I plan to continue my pulpit work.

Contact with the Northern Illinois District president, Dr. Ed Happel, led to immediate acknowledgment from the Missouri district president, Rev. Herman Scherer. I am informed that I am wanted, needed, and will be welcomed into the Missouri District. Some Missouri pastors write letters of welcome in case I should decide to come. More specifically, Dr. Happel informs me that according to what he knows I will be used extensively in Missouri. However, Dr. Happel also tells me that he wishes I had informed him earlier of the "strange" treatment at Concordia. Finally, I notify Concordia officials that I have received an offer to teach at Lincoln University in Jefferson City. I receive no response. Now my family comes with me to Jefferson City to see the house we are offered by the campus and near schools. Jean understands my feelings and agrees with me that I should accept the offer. We travel to Asheville, and from there I tender my resignation to the president of Concordia College, asking for a peaceful release to accept the professorship position at Lincoln University.

I return to the Concordia campus and just as suddenly as there seemed to have been a turn-the-head from me, heads are now turning towards me and asking if there is something they can do. Some are saying that they do not want me to leave and offer opportunity to resume teaching. I have a few hours to rethink and think again. If Lincoln University is to be canceled, I should tend to the matter this afternoon. At Concordia, there are those several persons who emphasize that I am needed here. Nonetheless, I have observed that particular individuals seem to consistently demonstrate personal unreadiness to accept me and/or the position described in my letter of appointment. Thus, I perceive a potential risk for the Concordia harmony experienced previously. There is this feeling that their offer should not be accepted. I decline. Finally, after efforts to discourage my leaving, administrators and colleagues wish me God's blessings.

10

A Blessed Period of Time: The Jefferson City Era

Foreshadowing

Scenes selected from my life for the nine foregoing chapters were memories shared in an almost chronological sequence. Age 6 in 1928 to age 48 in 1970 needed progressive representation. This chapter 10, my finale, departs from that pattern as I now form clusters of information sorted and summarized from August 1970 and thereafter through the 28th year, 1998, when I am completing my story.

The first information you will read is enlivened with family, the two houses, pets, and more. I have included a few briefs regarding our children from the day they arrived in Jefferson City through their live-at-home duration, specifically, high school graduation. Fortunately for all of us, Jean's duration continues. She completed her master's degree a few weeks before we arrived with fervent desire to become a full-time wife and mom for a few years. This is my desire too.

Also my salary is better than it was at Concordia College.

The greater focus of this final chapter provides glimpses of the road in later life in which my journey seems to continuously hold a pattern of the unforeseen as in previous years but with sharp contrasts. Now each of the unexpected that may astonish me is precisely a God-blessed experience, favorably minus the setbacks and disappointments. If justice could be given to only the summaries of my Jefferson City era, this chapter would require more pages than used for all of the book. Thus, for you, I have selected some items from my cargo of information.

Focusing on the Five Kings, Generally

In Jefferson City, we leased a recently built multilevel, brick home across the street from a section of the Lincoln campus. On day 1, as we were moving into the house, Jocelyn, Jann, and Roger were busy getting things into their rooms when Jean and I heard laments of gloom with doom. The threesome was huddled over the lease and reading it. "What?" "No pets again?" "The papers for the other places said no pets!" "Why no pets?" "We haven't had pets since we were in Chicago."

I was able to calm the anxiety a little when I told them that pets can come to the first house we own which will be this one if the owner will sell it. Then Roger asked if we could have a horse. I told him we would if possible. Jean and I had already decided that we should try to buy this place and that a letter will be written immediately to find out if the owner will sell. This was a beautiful family-style home on a large lot.

During the next two weeks our family was visited by pastors and some of the members of Jefferson City Lutheran churches. Each was inviting us to come to his/her church. During those same first days, I received preaching invitations from two of the churches. The Northern Illinois District president, Dr. Edmond Happel, was accurate in stating that I would find Missouri welcoming me as a clergyman in spite of my employment at a state institution. Surely, the news of our arrival reached Jefferson City churches, no doing of mine.

The owner of the house we leased answered my letter with a definite refusal to sell but granted us the privilege to break the lease as soon as we could acquire a house for sale. Immediately we began our search. Jean would work with real estate agents, ads, etc., and inform me of her progress during my lunch hours and at home in the evenings. Our preference was to find an adequate house on a large lot of about three acres in or near the area where we were living. Numerous houses met our criteria but none were for sale.

In one nearby location, there was a cluster of six vacant lots and two of them next to a small city park and a creek. We purchased those two lots, three acres, and had our house built. Very interesting, the creek, some woods, and the city park property were all that separated these lots from the house we were leasing.

We were nearly finished moving into our new home and still needed a few more hours in the "no-pets" house when Jocelyn brings a kitten she rescued, lost in a parking lot. She had already named her *Dolly*. This night of finishing moving was a little early for Dolly but we managed. Later, Jean and Jocelyn were finding homes for Dolly's litters of kittens. Then she was spayed. Roger's first dog, Dot, was found through a newspaper ad. He finally selected one of her puppies, Lil' Dot, for his dog to keep that he would train. Jann's friend asked her to keep a Siamese kitten for two weeks until the friend's friend came for it. Jann called him Chung. Chung's two-week stay lasted 15 years.

We had lived in Jefferson City for 10 months before moving into our own home. Our prayers that God would guide our family for housing were as serious as the prayers for guidance in other changes I felt directed to make. Also, I thought of the many moves we had made in the past seven years and now Jocelyn has one more year before graduation from high school. I concluded that the fourth bedroom would not be used for my den as first intended so that Jocelyn could have an adequate room of her own to design and enjoy during her senior year. Our move to Jefferson City had interrupted her matriculation at Walther Lutheran High School. She was making plans for her next year at Walther when we moved to Jefferson City.

Jocelyn seemed to have bravely gone along with a difficult change and kept remarkable composure when discussing her desire to have remained at Walther. But also remarkable was her adaptation to Jefferson City High School, where she displayed tremendous enthusiasm in continuing some of her former interests. She had been an excellent student in Latin for two years. Here she added Latin III and the Latin Club. An excellent performance in her English classes seemed easy for her, and she often said that she acquired her composition writing strength at Walther, where requirements were rigorous and writing was excessive. I admired her talent for leadership roles with the J. C. High yearbook staff, the Little Theater, and vocal music.

Her leadership with the Walther League at Faith Lutheran Church was commendable. She talked about trying to energize the members to be as motivated as her Walther League group at St. Paul Church, Melrose Park. We learned that some of the leaguers at Faith complained that their meetings were dull when Jocelyn was absent.

Both Jann and Roger enrolled in a public school, Thorpe Gordon, two blocks from our home for their fifth and second grades respectively. From grade 5 through high school, Jann showed talent and high interest in instrumental music, track, and infrequently, art. As she gave her interests more energy than could be afforded, she had to make special effort to avoid sacrificing her regular school subjects.

She had been enthusiastic for elementary orchestra with the violin until discovering woodwinds in grade 7. She tried a few and remained with alto saxophone, usually holding first chair in concert band during her senior year. The saxophone survived a rigorous girls' track team routine for all of her high school years. Often a winner, she posted a track record before graduation. For Jean and me, Jann's medals and wins had additional meaning—visible evidence of her blessed recovery from the crippling disease she had as an infant. I was unable to attend her track meets. Jean went and often tried to describe how she breathed a prayer of thanks to God when she watched Jann sail swiftly and easily around the track.

After two days in a Jefferson City public school classroom for second grade, Roger began to complain. He told us that he wanted to go to Trinity Lutheran School. His plea was voiced frequently until the end of the school year. He had been enrolled in Lutheran schools for kindergarten and first grade. In contrast to the previous schools, Trinity school's tuition seemed very high.

His second grade teacher described the same concern for Roger as was reported at Grace School in River Forest. His reading was still exceptional but he showed little motivation to write. She explained that in her 30 years of teaching, this was the first time she had provided fifth-grade books to meet a second-grade student's reading ability. But she also admonished us that Roger would be given D's in reading until he wrote in the second-grade workbook.

Tuition rules changed and Roger attended Trinity school grades 3 through 8. At his eighth-grade graduation, the principal cited how the students ranked according to classroom work and also standardized scores. While Roger's classwork did not receive honors, he was ranked among and/or above the top three students in reading, social studies, and word knowledge.

Roger's participation in Trinity's band was followed with four years of playing the snare drum for the marching band and serving as drum captain while playing various percussion instruments for concert band. He also served as timpanist for the orchestra.

Jann's and Roger's rites of confirmation took place at Faith Lutheran Church while Dr. Kalthoff was pastor.

Clergy Work

As aforementioned, preaching invitations were extended during my first week in Jefferson City. Following those initial requests, which I accepted, I began to receive invitations from various churches throughout Missouri. The occasions were usually anniversaries, mission festivals, and other special observances. I remained an intermittent participant in Lutheran ministerial activities for the duration of my tenure at Lincoln University.

I served as vacancy pastor for St. John's Lutheran churches of Schubert and Babtown and later for Immanuel Lutheran Church, Honey Creek. Both towns are areas of Jefferson City. Also during the '70s, Concordia Seminary invited me to teach two courses, evenings. "Teaching Christian Adults in the Parish" and "The Church's Ministry to Minorities." During the same semester, I provided consultation to the seminary in the area of continuing education and met with various students on the campus. In 1988 the seminary asked me to design a course for the doctor of ministry students, "Techniques and Strategies for Ministers Teaching Adults." I have taught the course three times since its inception. Also by request I designed a course for undergraduates, "Ethnic Ministries of the Church in North

America." I have taught this course most semesters through 1997. Also in 1997 I designed and taught "Urban Ministries Involving African Americans."

Lincoln University

Along my way at Lincoln, three interesting responsibilities were thrust upon me, (1) serving a three-year term as an elected member of the Jefferson City School Board; (2) the university marshal; (3) teaching and developing adult education. For the school board, I was encouraged by an official at the university and some of the community people inclusive of members of the Lutheran churches. It was encouraging to greet a noteworthy number of Lutherans at the nomination-night event, a tradition, now ended, that was partisan. On that particular evening, persons voting for Democrat nominees assembled in a school gymnasium as did the Republicans in a different location. Results were announced on the same evening.

The position as university marshal for eight years presented frequent interaction with the community, especially the public schools. There was specific involvement when coordinating homecoming activities, commencements, and honor assemblies.

My teaching was primarily graduate courses in the Department of Education while gradually developing an adult-education program. The salary was paid by the university, which also furnished the physical facilities for the adult-education activities. Funds for personnel and equipment were necessarily secured through the grants for which I wrote many proposals. In the first semester, I wrote a proposal generating $74,000. Acquisition of funds through proposals continued for 17 years, the time of my retirement from the university. I have conservatively estimated that $800,000 were acquired for the adult-education thrusts during my

146

tenure. Programs that I developed and implemented included the master's degree in adult education, GED satellites in various counties surrounding Jefferson City, a nine-state summer workshop for teacher training, institutes and short-term workshops, youth programs, and adult clerical skills programs that assisted participants with securing employment.

During my last five years at Lincoln University, there were occasions when I needed to travel because of my need to be involved with a church function in another city. To avoid canceling a class, I invited Jean to be my guest teacher for those classes. I had listened to the presentations she had done for my students in previous years and never doubted that she would do a very adequate job. She had received her doctoral degree in education from the University of Missouri in 1982, and therefore met the criteria to substitute for me. When Jean was invited by a UMC professor to pursue a doctoral degree, she showed surprise and indecision. I pointedly encouraged her to go for it. She says she did it upon my insistence. It is not so simply put. We gave this idea a prayerful vigil also. We both took time to really think and feel God's guidance. We are confident that God directed this decision.

My retirement from Lincoln University occurred at the end of the spring semester 1987. With many persons and some incentives presenting reasons to remain two or three more years, I felt that I should walk out at age 65. Thoughts of remaining a while longer included consideration for emeritus status and participation in the forthcoming retirement package that would provide an annual cost-of-living increase exceeding the pension promised if I left at age 65. However, other concerns seemed to hold priority, beckoning me to leave the university as quickly as possible. Various facets of churchwork were generating demands that could not be met if I remained at Lincoln. Each had either already begun or was waiting to be initiated soon as I would retire. Currently, ongoing, there was the work for Pilgrim Lutheran Church since 1977, speaking engagements, teaching intermittently at Concordia Seminary, and serving as third vice-president of The Lutheran Church—Missouri Synod as of 1986. Waiting since early 1986 was the Lay Ministry Program of Concordia College, Selma, for which I would be the director. For purposes here, the above concerns are not discussed in the same order.

Churchwork Increasing

The vice-presidency had overlapped with my last year at Lincoln. Early in 1986 I received a telephone call informing me that my name had been surfaced to be a vice-president of The Lutheran Church—Missouri Synod. The caller reiterated that the only African American vice-president was the Rev. Joseph Lavalais, who died while in office serving as fourth vice-president. I was asked to please consider. But for reasons which I am not sure, I gave few thoughts to the idea. Within two weeks I was called again but I offered no acceptance. While attending the next Black Clergy meeting in Memphis, all of the participants asked my consideration with assurance that I would have their endorsement at the upcoming convention the following summer, 1986.

During the convention, I was elected third vice-president; in 1989 at the convention in Wichita, I was elected second vice-president and re-elected at the 1992 convention in Pittsburgh. The same was repeated in 1995 in St. Louis. At this last election I was nominated for first vice-president and remained on the ballot among a number of names until the last three were considered. For the election of second vice-president, I received more than 900 votes, reportedly more than any candidate in the church's history. The source person for this information stated that 1,100 persons were participating as voters. I am expressing my true feelings about these election phenomena. God wanted to bestow the responsibilities upon me and therefore with His Spirit worked through the people to accomplish it. I continuously give God the praise and the glory!

The vice-presidency has been characterized by a variety of responsibilities. For some of the years, my assignments have been multidimensional. In representing the synodical president at district conventions, I travel to various states, East Coast to West Coast. My responsibilities include delivering the main sermons and special reports on synodical matters. I have also been involved according to appointment by the president to be his representative for the Boards of Regents of the two seminaries, the International Lutheran Women's' Missionary League (ILWML) and the International Lutheran Laymen's League (ILLL). I still serve for each with the exception of one of the Boards of Regents.

One year before my retirement from Lincoln University, Dr. Richard Dickinson of the Commission on Black Ministry informed me that the commission had planned to co-sponsor a lay ministry program with and for Concordia College, Selma. I had already served as a consultant for initial planning, but when asked to serve as director, I affirmed that such would be impossible while working at the university. Later, there were other times that he called to tell me, "I'm waiting on your retirement. How soon?" After retirement, I served as the director from 1987 to 1990. The work required professional, education program planning applied to lay-ministry purposes. At this point I am citing that educational program planning with implementation and evaluation was a major emphasis in my doctoral studies at Indiana University.

During the three lay-ministry years, with the supporting leadership of Dr. Dickinson and Rev. James McDaniels, I developed and evaluated at least 30 workshops conducted in cities including St. Louis, Pittsburgh, Philadelphia, New York City, Los Angeles, New Orleans, Chicago, and, especially, Selma. The total attendance was approximately 550 persons. A primary purpose was to recruit lay persons to pursue courses training them for lay-ministry responsibilities. We were able to initiate courses at Concordia College, Selma, on Friday afternoons through noon on Saturdays. I served as the instructor and asked Dr. Dickinson to replace me for some of the sessions. Later, I learned that some of our students began assisting in their parishes while others began to pursue courses in theology at our seminaries. God blessed graciously!

It is marvelous to behold the reality that this school in Selma was not closed as was once discussed. What if Immanuel Lutheran Seminary could have remained open also? I believe that we would be realizing a significantly larger number of well-prepared pastors than we currently have.

In 1992, I was asked to serve as a special recruiter for Concordia Seminary. Recruitment sites were targeted in Alabama, Georgia, Illinois, Louisiana, Michigan, Ohio, Wisconsin, and other states where there were apparent efforts to recruit more African American students to study for the holy ministry. Responses from the various sites ranged from zero to 60. Appeals were made to young, old, older, male, and female. I told the girls of the variety of church worker opportunities for them, especially in teaching and training as deaconesses. Results of the efforts are still being noticed several years later. At various times, I have learned of persons I contacted who are considering or entering the seminary. May God continue to bless the efforts and bring forth fruit!

Summarily, for Concordia Seminary I have served and still serve as guest professor, special recruiter, and sometimes speaker for chapel service. My last chapel service was conducted in the new St. Timothy and St. Titus Chapel. For me there seemed to have been solemnity with a spiritual uplift in that chapel, but above all, the Spirit of God was working through His Word.

Africa

Pilgrim Lutheran Church kindly permitted me to take a trip to Africa, Feb. 17, through March 10, 1989. I was accompanied by Rev. James McDaniels and Dr. Richard Dickinson, who also ably served as an assistant guide inasmuch as he had previously visited places to be included in the trip. We were invited by Dr. Nelson Unwene, president of the Lutheran Church of Nigeria.

Our plane landed in Northern Nigeria at Kano. As we descended the ramp, I saw a scene that vividly contrasted with what is usually seen in the United States. Instead of a mixture of colors of people, I beheld a sea of black faces with very few white persons dispersed throughout the crowd. We were met by a missionary and his delegation who drove us to a compound with a stone wall. Travel began the next day.

We drove 400 miles to Jos, where the host missionary served a congregation, the only church we had in this area of Nigeria. Also in Jos is Hillcrest, a school for children of expatriates and other missionaries. In this city, there were mansions and very good houses. People were as well dressed as would be seen in the average American city.

Our Synod had approximately 300 congregations in Nigeria with a total membership of 65,000 or perhaps 75,000 members. On one occasion, we were with the missionaries and their families from the United States—about 45 persons including the children at a five-day retreat. Our retreat site was within a guarded compound. I listened to the wife of a missionary who talked desperately of going home. I heard similar conversations, from three other wives with whom I talked. I offered serious encouragement reminding them of Jesus and His love, and in turn tried to persuade them to view their husbands' mission and ministry with more comforting insight.

Dr. Unwene had arranged for me to teach a one-week intensive course at Obet Idim Seminary. The course was "Principles of Teaching Christian Adults." I have never taught brighter students than the 15 young men who were enrolled in this course. They were perceptive, knowledgeable, and very astute.

A striking awakening was the information that missionaries are not in charge of the congregations. They serve as advisors, consultants, and translators of the Bible into some of the languages of certain people. Natives who speak English assist with the translating. Once in a Sunday worship service, we heard the Lutheran liturgy sung in the native language of the worshipers. We were able to join them but used English. At this church, the pastor preached the sermon in English. During the offering, the parishioners moved in line in the aisle using rhythmic steps to the tempo of instruments and drums to lay their offering upon the altar and return to their places with the same almost-dance style movements. For Communion, they clapped and strutted, approaching the Lord's Table.

Ground transportation was an on-going scene I would never have imagined. Everyone drove very fast and there were only a few traffic lights. In the city of Lagos I saw extremely few traffic lights and high speed was the custom. There were sometimes traffic jams, a convenience for peddlers to approach car windows to sell loaves of bread, chickens (alive or killed) and other goods. Beggars also approached cars during slow-speed moments. It was amazing that with people driving in the city, 60 to 70 miles an hour, I never saw a wreck. Certainly my greatest relief was that our Christian hosts always prayed when they got into their cars. This was true for each time that I rode in a car. The driver always waited until there was prayer. I recall hearing, "Let's pray. Dr. King or someone please lead us in prayer." Could the U.S.A. consider this prayer concept when operating vehicles?

The trip afforded priceless enlightenment and education about this section of Africa that I did not have because of my own neglect to stay current and the apparent biased information via media. In 1950, there were only two cities in Africa that had more than 1 million residents. During the time of my trip, there were 37 cities with populations exceeding 1 million. According to information provided by our Christian guide, in 1985 the world's most populous countries were China, India, Russia, and the United States. By the year 2012 the most populous countries will be China, India, Nigeria, and Pakistan. Nigeria will rank third in population. In 1989, one-fourth of the population of Africa was in Nigeria and the Christian church in Africa was then growing at the rate of 16,000 members each day. It is predicted that by the year 2000 there will be 393 million Christians in Africa, more than the population of the United States and Canada combined.

I enjoyed the realization of flying over the Sahara Desert, speculated to be large enough to hold the United States. Also, of great interest was my recall from childhood books about the Nile River, where the baby Moses was hidden, Egypt, and the Red Sea. I do not remember understanding or ever reading that those places were in Africa. Names of those places mentioned during the trip caused me to consider the inherent omission of Africa's relevance during my earlier schooling. I am thinking that it was perhaps during my graduate studies that I first read literature that precisely cited Africa as related to Bible history.

Pilgrim Church, a Special Era within an Era

From the beginning, Pilgrim Lutheran Church kept a congenial and mutual understanding that I would serve as a worker-priest (part-time, with full-time employment continuing at Lincoln University). Many small congregations have pastors who are worker-priests. The elders of the Pilgrim congregation informed me that their expectations would be Sunday morning preaching, youth confirmation class during the Sunday school hour, Baptisms, hospital calls, and funerals. I would not be required to make regular pastoral calls on members or conduct any evening or weekday activities except voters' assembly meeting at least once or twice a year.

It was soon discovered that Pilgrim had an admirable make-up unlike any church I had served or heard of. While the familiar Germanic ancestry was not unusual, as well as the location in a rural area, the church had unique characteristics that are not always seen in churches. There were about 50 adult members, total. They operated in a smooth synchronized pattern, making significant accomplishments with nearly every member always participating. Their system had and still has precision comparable to a small organized corporation. Most important, the love of Christ is very apparent in the harmony among the members. I often heard various persons say that this is the Lord's work. They are very perceptive and cooperative when rallying to meet various needs and emergencies.

Pilgrim is exceptional when compared with many churches regarding indebtedness. The members give generously towards having no money owed on a building when it is finished. There was no debt on the recently built edifice when I became their pastor. It was marvelous to observe the beautiful brick multipurpose building erected debt-free at the time of completion. This was accomplished through financial contributions from the parishioners. Also noteworthy about the multipurpose building is that the members, not the pastor, initiated the idea, did the planning, and monitored the fund raising. Instead of prayerfully, carefully helping to lead the endeavor as I did in three other churches, I prayerfully, joyfully supported.

Instead of describing Pilgrim as a rural church, it seems more appropriate to state that it is a suburban church that happens to be located on an expansive and beautiful acreage in the rural town of Freedom. The church building is brick and looks brand-new. To many first-time visitors, the impressive interior is a surprise. It is inspirational—with cathedral-style ceiling; dark walnut trim; sculptured, walnut-paneled chancel with matching furnishings; and custom-built pews. Very churchly.

Being a person desirous to serve a small congregation, Pilgrim was a very compatible fit for me. No problems and circumstances occurred that needed my weekday time and concentration. Nonetheless I gave serious concentration to implanting my mind with ideas that could be used to enhance my ministry whenever I left the university. Therefore, upon my Lincoln University retirement, I immediately asked the members for cooperation for one of my ideas, a serious evangelism effort. An evangelism committee was formed. Also, I worked some weekdays in the community making calls on those few members who did not attend regularly, and I had serious person-to-person contact with persons who were unchurched. Some of Pilgrim's members gave me names to contact, usually resulting in gaining new members. I traveled through the church's community, visiting the shut-in members more often and persons who had indicated interest in the church.

Gradually, I was increasing my time far beyond the original part-time concept, but this was my own desire. I prayed daily for the Lord's blessings and guidance as I continued to work for the church.

Some of the members were enthusiastic to keep the choir active. I joined them, using my tenor voice best that I could. The congregation had not been using the "Order of Matins." The choir, upon my suggestion, rehearsed it and led the congregation in singing this liturgy.

In the mid 1980s, the members of the 1979 youth group were now young adults. We used two of the new confirmation classes to begin a second group. I asked Jean to serve as leader temporarily, and I would assist her with hope that we would soon have two persons appointed who were willing to serve. The group of four had its own unofficial name, "Teen Action," which seemed to have special appeal to teenagers. To provide more opportunity for outdoor games, the four teens who were members were encouraged to invite friends. There were nine teenagers attending some of the meetings. Our late Sunday afternoon meetings monthly did not interfere with the visiting teens' church hours. In 1996, I saw 14 teenagers in a meeting, all of whom were members of our congregation. To God be the glory!

Nineteen-ninety-four was an eventful evangelistic year. I asked the members to pray and work with me towards adding 30 additional souls to our membership. I gave my prayerful, concentrated efforts, and the members cooperated also. On the last Sunday in December, we received the 30th person into the congregation's membership. God is worthy to be praised. That Sunday in December is memorable and cherished. This 30-person increase had not been any easy accomplishment. Significant weekday time was used especially for giving membership instructions in some of the homes. I had used home instruction for many of the members of Victory Church in Youngstown. Most of them remained faithful. Even though I sometimes provide instructions in the home, the family member(s) for whom the sessions are aimed are expected to attend the church services while taking instructions. There have been situations wherein a visiting friend or relative would join the home discussions and later become a member.

Another glorious year was 1993, when Pilgrim's 125th anniversary was observed. The Rev. Dr. Oswald Hoffmann was our guest preacher for the morning worship and the outdoor service in the afternoon. The day was glorious and festive. Music included the Sweet Spirit Trio from St. Mark's Lutheran Church, Eureka, two Pilgrim teenage instrumentalists with flute and trumpet, and our choir. A new array of banners was on display. During this occasion, our new multipurpose facility was dedicated to provide more space for children and youth activities.

Pilgrim Church members were personally kind to Jean and me all of the time. For the years 1979 and 1989, they prepared dinners celebrating our 30th and 40th wedding anniversaries and my 30th and 40th years in the holy ministry. Both occasions are still well remembered. They also kindly supported my out-of-the-parish activities and absences that occurred because of my vice-presidential responsibilities. Also, my teaching ministry at the seminary was approved and encouraged.

On the afternoon of my last Sunday as pastor, and ending my 20th year, the congregation held an open house reception in the undercroft of the church. Those in attendance included members, friends from the community and nearby Lutheran churches, the circuit counselor, and other Lutheran pastors. I was presented an elegant plaque of a 12-inch brass Missouri Synod cross mounted on sculptured walnut wood. This cherished keepsake hangs by my favorite chair in our living room.

Retirement?

My retirement from Pilgrim occurred in the midst of some of my teaching and other ministry responsibilities from which I was not retiring. My last Sunday at Pilgrim was six days after my course ended at Concordia Seminary and 10 days before I would begin intensive travel for five conventions, four days each serving as the president's representative. Within four weeks I would travel to River Forest, Ill.; Minnesota; Montana; Washington; and Charlotte, N.C. Jean accompanied me to River Forest and Charlotte.

Prior to the onset of the conventions, Jean and I took out time to celebrate our 48th wedding anniversary. We had not done anything very special since our 45th, for which the family held a celebration in Chicago in 1994.

July 1997 held the days that I had looked forward to completing most of this book. Impossible. I promised Dr. Eugene Bunkowske that the summer of 1997 would be the earliest time I could have to teach a course at Concordia Theological Seminary, Fort Wayne, Ind. The intensive two-week course was developed for students in the doctoral program. It required all of July for teaching, handling evaluations, and reading/scoring student papers. On the first weekend of the course I was able to schedule a quick round trip to Atlanta and make a scheduled presentation for the Black Ministry Convocation.

Aug. 1 found Jean and me at the King Family Reunion in Knoxville, Tennessee, hosted by my youngest sister, Janice Robinson and her family. This was a happiness-filled event, Friday through Sunday.

Can Angels Laugh?

Jean is saying that my guardian angel was laughing when the family reunion closed. On our way home on Sunday, we both talked about my trip to St. Louis, which would be the next day. I would be attending the International Theological Convocation. Intermittently, I commented on the feeling of just attending and enjoying an affair without being required to make any presentations. I said that there is much satisfaction in not needing to prepare anything for this occasion. I was especially looking forward to meeting and talking with theologians from other nations as well as those of the U.S.A. and Canada during the reception on Monday and continuously during the days following.

On Tuesday, I walked into the International Theological Convocation area a few minutes before the opening and was presented an activities schedule. At one glance my name seemed to appear two or more times on each page. Certainly I showed surprise and spoke with much astonishment. Immediately, one of the chief officials apologized, expressing serious concern that I did not receive notification by mail. The prepared agenda indicated that I was the chaplain of the convocation, conducting all openings and closings for each day and prayers before meals. I was due in the auditorium for the first devotion immediately.

Throughout the three days, a noteworthy number of visiting theologians clamored to give their attention to the messages in my presentations, generally, and some cited specific concepts that were meaningful for them. Also, I really felt that God and I accomplished the assignment very appropriately. My angel laughing? Jean said that my guardian angel knew what I would have done if the convocation booklet had reached me before we left for the reunion. The angel knew that if I had known my plight, many enjoyable family moments would have been used by me in our hotel room, jotting down notes for each meditation. She said that my guardian angel also knew that God has already prepared me more than I seem to realize. Herewith a husband is publicly admitting that his wife is right about what he would have done. She laughed even if the angel didn't.

There were activities listed for both of us on our fall 1997 calendar. Jean continued to temporarily serve with the

Pilgrim youth group and conduct the youth Bible class. She expects to be replaced soon. She has continued her one day weekly at Drury. The seminary course I taught ended November 10 and another begins March 8 of this year, 1998. The vice-presidential duties and speaking engagements appear to be ever present. Jean accompanies me for some occasions. One of my speaking responsibilities in December was for the fall commencement at Concordia University in Austin, Tex.

Reflecting on the prologue of my story, retirement time is continuing to afford some surprise demands. But as stated, this is not a complaint. Circumstances find me scampering posthaste. Am I enjoying retirement? YES! How pleasant to retire under the shepherding of God whose grace never retires. It is by God's grace for Christ's sake, through faith, that I am who I am. I am a child of my heavenly Father, a minister of my redeeming Savior, and an heir of eternal life under the sustaining power of the Holy Spirit. As God wills it by His never-failing grace, I will continue to believe, live, love, and serve until He grants me a blessed departure in peace.

The calendar shows February 1998, and I am boldly abandoning this assignment of writing my life's story. It was a pleasurable task. Reliving my life in writing inevitably sets forth the words through which my hope and strength receive joyful renewal. These words were spoken by Jesus for all of us, and I have shared with you as Pastor Jenkins said to me, "Seek ye first the kingdom of God and His righteousness, and all these things shall be added unto you" (Matthew 6:33).

Certainly, I was born into the riches of God's grace. Nobody told me that I was born into poverty.

11

Now, Jean

This section was requested by the author and some of our close friends who knew that the book was in progress. Why? They have all said that it is something I should do, no specific reason given. How does a wife develop a chapter for her husband's autobiography? I'm thinking we are pioneering. With imagination and nobody's guidelines but mine, I looked forward to an enjoyable task.

I imagined questions you, the reader, may have had about the Jean that Robert surfaces or discusses in some of his chapters. Therefore, I perceived this as an opportunity to briefly provide glimpses of me before meeting Robert and after. Also, I have included why I did not answer his last letters "once/twice upon a time."

Robert mentions the reluctance with which I gave him my Asheville, N.C., address. This was not the usual me. Generally, I would add that my city was also called the beautiful "Land of the Sky," up, inside, and high within the Great Smokies. On this first face-to-face with Robert, I felt somewhat inhibited to continue our discussion. I will divulge more on that meeting later.

Asheville, "the Land of the Sky," was my hometown

since birth with the exception of ages 5 to 10 when Daddy tried farming. We moved from Asheville to a small farm and made three moves to other farms not far from each other during this five-year period. All of the time we were only about 10 miles from Asheville. Therefore, we sometimes returned for shopping or to see the annual Rhododendron Parade. Transportation was our car at first, then a wagon with one horse, and later, a truck Daddy bought with his delayed veterans' bonus money. He was a World War I veteran.

I was the third of five children with an older brother and sister, Lloyd and Ruth, and a younger brother and sister, Thomas and Ellen. We did not have the rewarding advantages of living nearby grandparents, aunts, uncles, and cousins as Robert's family had. Our grandparents lived in other states. Mama's mother was in New York, and Daddy's mother and father lived in Lincolnton, Ga., on the farm where Daddy lived until he married and moved to Asheville. Mama was from Greenwood, S.C., and met Daddy when she was teaching at Mt. Zion School in Lincolnton. This was the job to which she was appointed after graduating from Brewer Normal Institute in Greenville, S.C.

In the country, one of our houses was near two children. Our playmates were generally our own family members. I have always recalled those days as some very good times. We played traditional childhood games with each other. Also, there was the fun of telling stories that had been read and there were many books all of the time. Our favorites were read and talked about repeatedly. Some of our books were sent by Mama's sister, who was a teacher in New York.

Several years into my adulthood, Daddy told me that when I was six years old, he sometimes told me to read "The Lost Kitten" story to him again. He said he only did this to watch the tears roll down my cheeks when I read the section about the kitten crying, running all over the barnyard and unable to find its mother. He said that my voice never changed as I kept reading, but the tears dried as the kitten and its mother were reunited. Daddy said that he could not keep his secret from me any longer. I only remember reading the story often with no memory about any tears.

Homework was a family session in our house. Everybody knew what each was studying. Mama looked over all of the English and spelling and coached memory work. Daddy helped with arithmetic when needed.

I really liked the outdoors, which caused me to hang around Daddy and my older brother, Lloyd, when they were repairing things outside. Lloyd also took me with him when he went to pick blackberries on the side of the mountain. Sometimes, we picked three gallons of berries.

Home was a real haven for me during my first few years of school life because my grade-level girl classmates found ways to hurt me nearly every day during recess. I enrolled in the Concord Elementary School at age 5 in the first grade. This was a one-room school building. My classmates were older, and much larger. Our family members were the outsiders coming into this established rural community. The teacher told the children that I was an advanced reader and asked me to help them with difficult words. Outside, the girls would jerk me and sometimes punch me until I cried. I would tell the teacher while the girls all declared it wasn't true. Mama urged me to try and stay in the sight of Lloyd and Ruth when I was outdoors, and that I should not "fight back." I'm sure she understood that I was outnumbered.

During our stay at three different places in this community, the "head" lady of the little church and the community asked Mama to prepare children's programs for Easter, Christmas, and Children's Day. This lady, Mrs. Lynch, seemed to sense the innate aura of caring that characterized my mother. She also knew that Mama had the abilities needed. This was a first for this little church to order programs. Mama selected David C. Cook Church Publishers. Her programs were welcomed by the community residents with many statements of gratitude. I was unaware that years later, I would also order materials—but from Concordia Publishing House—and develop children's Christmas pageants.

Buncombe County closed our school, and I began to ride my first school bus. We enrolled in the Arden School, three rooms and three teachers, where I completed grades 3 and 4. Here the classmates from my first school did not touch me anymore. They only laughed at my lunches, exclaiming that my sandwiches were made with biscuits instead of store-bought bread. Once, annually, the school competed with several other county schools for prizes for chorus, drama, spelling, and mathematics. My brothers, sister, and I caused our school to earn at least two blue ribbons each year.

The county closed Arden, and I rode a bus to Shiloh Elementary School, much closer to Asheville than the previous schools. There were seven grades and seven teachers. A special happiness for me at Shiloh was my girlfriend, Virginia, who had always attended this school. She adopted me into her friendship group. Outdoor recess time was fun and a really good time for me. The girls from my former school stayed together; they seemed very unhappy in our "new" school. I was destined to attend the Shiloh school for fifth grade only. We would move back to Asheville. Serious farm failure had prevailed. Daddy's prior knowledge of farming was limited to low-altitude crops such as cotton and watermelons. For mountain productivity, he refused to follow the free advice of the agriculture extension agents and farm journals. Mama used both sources for a productive garden and unusually outstanding chickens.

My sister, Norma Ellen, was born in January of the year

we were to move from the country. I was 10 years older than she and was permitted to help Mama with her. I enjoyed rocking her to sleep, for which Mama kept close watch because I usually fell asleep also, and she needed to lift Ellen and place her on the bed. I had not been allowed to help with my brother, Thomas. I was only two and a half when he was born. The close watch Mama kept then was to stop me when I would sneak and pull him out of the bed. Thomas was born the year that my grandmother sent a large brown doll, Big Ann. At first I was frequently pointing to Thomas and saying, "Another Big Ann." It all started when he was one day old and I discovered the "doll" in the bed with Mama.

Moving back to Asheville caused me to relinquish fun with my farm pets. I had been permitted to claim any of the chicks, ducks, and piglets as mine. I enjoyed treating them as pets. It was always disappointing when each cow chased me from her calf. Also, very unpleasant was Daddy scolding me for sitting in the hog pen playing with my pig, Pee Wee. I would only be allowed to feed him.

Now, I was looking forward to indoor plumbing and electricity again. But I had never regretted working (playing) with our oil lamps. I usually asked to completely "refurbish" a lamp without help, washing it, adding the kerosene, trimming the wick, and polishing the chimney. Perhaps Mama knew I would like to have our special family lamp, and gave it to me. Today, in 1998, I still have it with plenty of memories that include doing homework with its light.

In Asheville, I completed elementary school. Lloyd, my brother, was attending a high school in New Haven, Conn., where he lived with Mama's sister, Aunt Sara, and helped in her funeral home on weekends and some evenings. Daddy was reemployed at the Veterans Hospital, and Mama began to sew for some of her former customers as well as do domestic work for a previous employer.

At age 12, I enrolled in Stephens Lee High School, where my sister Ruth was already a senior. We walked six blocks to the school, a beautiful three-story brick building on a hill. I was not in perfect harmony with algebra and geometry, but there was always easy accord with English, music study (a structured music-appreciation course), and Latin. Students did not choose to take Latin. The top scorers on a standardized English test were told to enroll in Latin. Others were to wait for the junior year and take French.

Hair can produce amusing and interesting conversations. Ruth's hair was about the same as that of two of our grandparents. It was naturally straight, flowing sleek, shoulder length with few waves. My hair was crimpy and had refused to grow. Therefore, I entered high school wearing four short braids tucked against my head. I frequently heard, "Why don't you have hair like your sister's?" Then there was the often-repeated statement, "She is much prettier than you." Two of my teachers made the same remarks on different occasions and the students laughed. Once, one of them added, "What happened to you?" During high school years, six of my courses were taken from those two teachers, who were overt in practices that I should be ignored regardless of good work while they gave special attention to students whose parents were in professional work or had high incomes as reflected in how their children dressed. Also, there were teachers who gave unbiased attention to all students. I always received better grades from those teachers.

During my second year in high school I was consistently involved in church. I joined the junior choir and began attending the Sunday evening Baptist Training Union (BYPU). Activities for those evenings were Bible study, Bible quiz competitions, and singing. This was Nazareth Baptist Church, which we attended before moving to the country.

My decision to join the church and be baptized differs

markedly from Robert's story of his Baptism in chapter 1. I was 14 when on a particular Sunday Ruth was in Sunday school and I was at home with a cold. She told me that she wished I could have attended on that day because the guest revival minister visited my Sunday school class, talked with the class members and exhorted them to accept Jesus Christ as their Savior, join the church, and be baptized after the revival. Each of the teenagers responded positively. They would not need to walk to the front of the church during service, as was the usual practice. Ruth urged me to unite with the church during the next few weeks before the Baptism and be baptized with my class.

During the next two weeks, on Sundays, I stood and sang with the congregation during the invitational hymn. My sister glanced toward me but did not say anything. Both of my parents had begun working on Sunday mornings. On one of those Sundays our pastor looked straight towards me and I pretended that his eyes did not meet mine. As usual, he was quoting some of Jesus' words from Mark 16:16, "He that believeth and is baptized shall be saved." The Baptism for the teenagers occurred without me. At home, I had often looked at our church's invitational hymn in one of our hymn books, "Softly and Tenderly Jesus Is Calling." Actually, I liked it and sang it for my own enjoyment.

I allowed a few months to pass and my 15th birthday passed also. I secretly decided when I would do it. Finally, on a Sunday, special for me, I stood and began to sing with the congregation as usual. I knew the words well. Today, it seemed that those words were being spoken to me. As I walked down the aisle towards the pastor he showed a friendly, faint smile, I glanced up at the choir that stood beneath the tall organ pipes. The choir was singing the last stanza as I reached the front of the church. Then I noticed some of the choir members looking at me and smiling. Ruth was not with me. She had returned to college. When my parents returned from work that same afternoon, I did not tell them what I had done. But I knew they would be very pleased, even relieved. On the following Tuesday, I told Mama; she smiled and said that she was really glad and added, "I noticed during the past two days that you have changed a lot. You are like a brand-new person." Within a few weeks, I was baptized with one other person in the church's baptismal pool beneath the floor, near the choir.

Also during age 15, while taking piano lessons, I finally pleased my mother by learning to play a hymn. Mama insisted that inasmuch as my piano lessons never required a hymn, she would reward me a quarter if I would learn to play any hymn in our family's hymnals. She told me that this was one step towards learning a skill that I might need some day. Her "some day" came within my next eight years as mentioned in chapter 6.

I graduated from high school in 1943, age 16, in a class of 100 students. I was in the honor society but far from the top of the class. Again, how amusing hair can be for some humans. The summer following my high school graduation, those two teachers I mentioned on a previous page and some of my classmates greeted me on the street, and each time used the name *Ruth*. They always seemed stunned when I identified myself. What had happened? My sister's idea was to style my hair swept up on the top of my head same as hers with curls on the forehead. She also made us each a dress exactly alike. Various persons who saw us together were surprised at the likeness. But as I noticed I was getting taller than Ruth, I began to slump. She and Mama rebuked me about my shoulder-slumping at once. I finally listened.

Ruth was attending Winston-Salem Teachers College, approximately 200 miles from Asheville. Whenever she was at home, she had never failed to tell me that I would find much more happiness in college than in high school. She would also state that my grades and behavior would be the important factors without elitism. She was right.

I enrolled in Barber-Scotia Presbyterian College for Women, fall 1943. On the first day, the Dean of Students talked with me when I arrived and asked me to return to her office after I settled into my room. She requested that I serve as her receptionist on the next afternoon, which would be Sunday. Later, a few upper-class students congratulated me, stating that Dean Cecil never assigned this responsibility to freshmen. The Dean heard them and told me, "My first impression when you entered the door was that you have the skills needed for this duty." Within a few months she assigned me a topic to develop for a Sunday morning chapel address. Surprise. This was also an assignment reserved for upper-class students. Following each Sunday morning chapel activity we were expected to attend the Presbyterian church near the school for worship.

The instructors at Barber-Scotia were very competent and generally demanded high standards for coursework. I made the honor roll both semesters, enjoyed loyal friendships, but transferred to Bennett College in Greensboro for my sophomore year. The transfer was made because Bennett was my intended school for the freshman year, but the enrollment was finalized early in the spring and I was sent an application to apply the next year. At Bennett College I would eventually meet the writer of this book.

Bennett was a women's college operated by the United Methodists. Church attendance was not required, but for the Sunday afternoon vespers seats were checked. Attendance was mandatory with a limited number of absences allowed each semester. Privately, in my room, I frequently read my tattered-edged, worn New Testament while sitting on my bed at night. There was no table beside the bed on which to place my New Testament. It stayed tucked barely beneath the mattress. I read it randomly. A printed meditation guide was not available. But I read with strong belief that Jesus Christ is my Savior.

One night I dreamed that a man was standing by my bed. He was tall, dressed, wearing a dark suit, with a white handkerchief folded with one point in the breast pocket. I saw no face, only the body in the suit. Clearly, I heard a female voice say, "That's your husband." This dream never occurred in my thoughts again until Robert and I had been married for two years and I was trying to rearrange the white pocket handkerchief into a different style for the fold. On the night of this dream at Bennett College, marriage was far from my thinking. When I was attending Barber-Scotia, one of my favorite instructors, Mrs. Ashton, who had a loving, happy family, admonished a few of us girls that we should remain Christian and pray that God would lead us to our husband of His choice. She cautioned us in this way more than a few times. She always added, "That's what I did." I heard her. More specifically, I listened. Nevertheless, whenever I prayed about the matter I asked God to please guide me to the right person in future years when I am perhaps 24 years old after a few years of work and graduate school. Then I would want to become a housewife full-time. If this seems crazy to my readers, I agree. But at that time I was serious. I thought God would hear my prayer as He had done previously: My lost wallet was found; I prayed and did well on some tests; and numerous times, He helped me with problems after prayer. Therefore, with such thoughts, I was to concentrate on college towards getting the task completed and not inclusive of any spouse search. I was confident about God's love and care, but perhaps my prayers needed "Thy will be done ..."

As I was growing up in my family, neither parent talked to us about marriage. Aims expressed usually dealt with education. All of us knew that college required work and sacrifice. Summer earnings were applied to tuition, and I had jobs at Barber-Scotia and at Bennett.

My major at Bennett was home economics, with a goal to specialize in child development. But this specialization was available only in graduate school and would have to wait. One of my hobbies was writing anything short for human interest. I was appointed reporter for Lyceum programs for the school newspaper; had fun winning each annual slogan contest; and finally, during my junior year, wrote a short story in the short story writing course, which was an elective. The instructor said it was the best student writing in all of his classes, including senior English majors. English course work at Bennett was not difficult because much of it was covered at Barber-Scotia. My first college, "Scotia," was small but had a reputation for being very advanced.

On a Sunday evening near the end of my junior year I met Robert King for the first time. He reports this meeting in chapter 5. I am herewith explaining my reluctance to give my address towards becoming his pen pal. His idea seemed strange because World War II, for which pen pals were a popular practice, was now ended. When my brother was in the Army, he permitted one of his friends to write to me, but that was history. Here, Robert stands in this dorm reception area, asking for my address, and I am trying to think, "Should I? Should I not?" When I did not answer his last letter late in August, I was remembering the formal, structured personality he seemed to have on the evening that we met. He seemed to have been a very serious person, diametrically the opposite from me. He had requested a summer pen pal. Our letter exchange was all right. Now summer is ended.

In September, he came to my dormitory to see me on a Saturday afternoon, fully dressed, dark suit, tie, and the white handkerchief that I would not yet recognize. He had the appearance and poise I would equate more with a faculty person than a student. And even though he was really a handsome man, I felt very mismatched for his type. Robert barely smiled and never laughed once during his visit that afternoon. He returned on another evening and I simply felt that he was such a good looking guy to be so solemn and quiet except for talking about his heavy course load of 21 semester hours.

This was my senior year, with student teaching in another city, Asheville, as well as all of the preparation for leaving. We did not see each other any more until the day on the train when he smiled easily and actually laughed about seeing my sister and me together and unable to recognize which was Jean. When he asked to write me again, I really felt better about correspondence than I did the last year. However, later in the summer I noticed that his letters expressed desire to see me again. I began to wish that I could introduce him to a girl as mature and formal as he seemed to be. I was realizing that this is a nice person that I do not want to hurt, and I was not the person for him. I would think about another letter when I go to Raleigh for my first teaching position. Ruth had typed at least 20 letters of application for teaching positions for me, and I had received only one affirmative response. I thanked God for it and was very eager to begin. Mama was especially thrilled and talkative about my prospective job with blind students.

Later in the fall when Robert spoke to me in the Greyhound Bus Terminal, chapter 5, I was the solemn one for a change because I was wondering what in the world had happened with him. He was overcast with a radiant countenance that was pleasantly contrary to the man I talked with in school. As I listened to him laugh and talk fluently, even happily, I was quietly trying to decide what to conclude. No conclusion except that he was really a likable person. Our friendship grew from that day as he explains in his writing. Also, a realization that I really loved him began growing with me.

Robert and I have discussed the situation that existed with him the year that we first met. This was less than a year since his critical, near-death illness. He had rushed full speed into school and was doing more thinking than talking and was definitely thinking about things he did not want to surface. We have agreed that during that first year, he was not "the old self." It is miraculous that he was able to successfully complete his over-the-limit course loads both semesters and summer. He never told me of his 1945 illness until a few months after we were married.

During our engagement, I was still a Baptist but willing to become a Lutheran. Robert introduced me to his pastor in Greensboro and stated that I would be attending the pastor's next membership class. Pastor Hunt responded with a hearty laugh and finally said, "You are near graduation. I know you have learned how to conduct the instructions. I'm assigning her to you." Robert blushed. He accepted the assignment. I was confirmed at Grace Lutheran Church a few weeks before our wedding vows.

Why did I choose the unbelievable hour of six o'clock in the morning for the marriage? My idea. I wanted the wedding to be held in a church, with all appropriate decorum, and could not afford it unless I waited and worked one more year. This was our lovers' quarrel. Robert had told me he could wait; now he could not. It was feasible for us not to delay, but I had first planned for the next year. He straightforwardly declared that whatever I arranged for the hour was all right with him. I was informed of a wedding held at six o'clock in the morning and I liked the idea inasmuch as it had to be in the home.

The reader of this book has probably noticed that during our first year of marriage I was able to bake an apple pie on our one-unit electric burner. There was a golden brown crust bottom, sides and top. I had never heard of the idea until I schemed it.

Robert's chapter 2 reports that when we moved to Jefferson City, I desired to stay out of the workforce for a few years. I enjoyed being full time with family and me. It was a comforting and blessed feeling to take time out alone during the day for prayer, concentration, and always asking God's help for family and house concerns. This was age 44, and I often enjoyed reading our *Little Visits with God* even though its primary purpose was to use for our family devotions. Finally, I was able to do more in the home.

My sewing machine and I have always been good friends. Finally, I employed it productively again. Its most important function was that it signaled Jocelyn and Jann to use it for some easy-to-make items. Roger also found many ways to stitch with it. I was able to become a volunteer helper for various activities in the children's three schools. Jann hosted her 11-member Girl Scout troop for an "over-nighter."

Mentioned earlier was the completion of my master's degree two weeks before we arrived in Jefferson City. Phenomenal experiences preceded and followed that degree. I actually believe that my overseeing angel prevailed with me to select guidance and counseling for my master's degree at Indiana University. The child development master's degree was temporarily on hold and other choices were not available. Also, I was under strong spouse encouragement to delay no longer. I felt that the counseling studies could help explain the counselor roles into which I was previously thrust without training.

During the college years, students frequently selected me to hear and discuss their personal problems. On one occasion, I told a student, "After we discuss yours, it's my turn to tell you mine." "No," she emphatically replied. "Everybody knows you don't have problems." I was unaware of casting such deception.

While teaching child development at a high school in Youngstown and later in Chicago, the principal of each of the schools asked me to allow my schedule to be readjusted so that I could assist with counseling. In each case it was noticed that various students voluntarily rushed to my classroom at the end of any day or stood outside the door waiting their turns. Yes, they had problems. Years later, many students at Lincoln University came to my office after certain topics were discussed in an orientation class or other course.

Several years after earning my doctoral degree and while teaching "Psychology of Human Growth and Development" at Drury College, the familiar pattern has not ceased. The clientele of my classes is mostly adults who are usually parents.

Did the counseling courses help my understanding? I actually learned more and was also relieved to discover that I was "on track" all of the time. In one of my classes, the professor asked, "Are counselors trained or born." After a few minutes of wild discussion he stated, "The first person to whom a student tells a personal problem is the student's counselor even if that person is the janitor."

My omniscient God is the source of any true knowledge I have gained through graduate studies. Through training and multitudinous experiences, He continues to refine my skills for helping people and also enables me through His Holy Spirit to discuss His saving grace and mercies with other individuals. When my self-referred clients come with problems, they appear to feel very at ease when I tell them that they are talking to a Christian.

We had lived in Jefferson City for two years before I earnestly sought part-time work with various agencies. When

I explained my aim to the Dean of Students at Lincoln University, he asked me to consider a counseling position of a new program being designed for student success. He promised that I could be excused for emergencies with our children. My office building was two blocks from our house when walking down hill and through the campus. I began the job in 1972 and ended it in 1992 when I began teaching in the Education Department for Drury College, full time but only three days weekly.

The reality remains that Robert instigated the new position. Upon his suggestion, I responded to a call for papers for the Missouri Association for Adult and Continuing Education (MAACE), an organization in which he still held membership. My proposal was accepted. After making my presentation at the MAACE convention, an administrator from Drury College talked with me and stated that such thinking could be used at Drury College. I expressed my interest in teacher education. The administrator asked me to send her my resume immediately.

I taught both graduate and undergraduate courses. Now, in semiretirement, I usually teach the human development course at Drury's closer campus.

Since 1992, I have served on the Board of Regents, Concordia, Selma. The marveling composition of chapter 3 is the author's matriculation at the Alabama Lutheran Academy in Selma. This academy, the institutional transition through which Concordia College became a significant reality, is one of my joy-filled reflections as I serve on the Board of Regents.

For reasons, I am finally citing one of Robert's characteristics omitted in his story. He is a "roses" man. For most special days, he has brought or sent red roses, one dozen, more, or less. Roses have appeared for most birthdays, Mother's Day, and anniversaries. Once, he left them in the kitchen when Jocelyn was four. When I read his note to give one to her, she acted with terror that Daddy only allowed one for her. As I tried to quiet her and explain that we are married and today was an anniversary, she only cried more telling me, "I want to be married too."

Did you notice that I have not addressed any of the details of my activities in the churches that Robert served? His chapters 6, 7, and 10 present significant paragraphs in which the two of us worked both individually and as one in his ministry. He has surfaced my involvement as it really was. Was the role difficult for me? NO! I was using my abundance of God-given skills. These were compounded daily with additional skills gained from experiences into which He cast me. I enjoyed the accomplishments and the required work. All along the way I often prayed that my efforts were made through faith in Jesus' name and to His glory. Otherwise my thrusts would have been in vain.

Postscript

There is a friend with whom I sometimes discussed my progress with this autobiography. When the writing was nearly completed, he made a challenging inquiry, "Is there a word to our younger contemporaries from you, the experienced pastor and teacher?" This thought-arousing question determined these next paragraphs.

As a Pastor

PREACH

We may be gifted in several abilities and subject areas, but we should remain mindful that it has "pleased God by the foolishness of preaching to save them that believe" (1 Corinthians 1:21). Basic to being an effective pastor is to "preach the Word" (2 Timothy 4:2). Our sermons must be Scripture-based, using both Law and Gospel, communicated in language understandable by the hearers.

STUDY

When I was a vicar under Dr. Marmaduke Carter, I asked him to kindly share some of his words of wisdom.

Looking directly into my eyes, he said, "Study, Son, study." After a pause he continued, "Study to shew thyself approved unto God, a workman that needeth not to be ashamed, rightly dividing the word of truth" (2 Timothy 2:15). I can give young pastors no better advice than the admonition received from Dr. Carter. While being diligent students of the Scriptures and the Confessions of the church, we should certainly seek enlightening resources with journals, videos, audiotapes, and computer assistance to enable us to learn the maximum possible towards equipping God's people in faith, love, and service.

EMPATHY

We are to become one of the people to whom we are ministering in whatever the circumstances experienced. The effective minister addresses people's needs and interests with no attempt to "clone" them into the pastor's image. He remains the undershepherd for the "sheep." With faith and love for the Savior, the two are molded together inseparably even when there are problems. The late Dr. Henry Nau often told seminary students, "Avoid cracking the whip to frighten the people; don't try to drive them like cattle; lead them as a shepherd his sheep." I do not intimate that a pastor become used or abused. The people are to show love, honor, and respect to their pastor as a servant of Jesus Christ.

FAMILY

A vital asset to a pastor is his family, especially his wife. Married pastors and their wives are tied into oneness and togetherness by holy wedlock. They can work and serve as partners together with Christ in His service. I have seen many men and women fall from heights to valleys because of nonsupportive spouses. "If a house be divided against itself, that house cannot stand" (Mark 3:25). The pastor's home is to be a Christian haven and workplace for the whole family.

Within the work, companionship, fun, and problems, the popular inscription seen on many wedding gifts is important: "Christ is the head of this house, the unseen guest at every meal, the silent listener to every conversation." A gift from the late Rev. and Mrs. Walter Werning, a plaque bearing those words, has hung in our kitchen since 1949.

As a Teacher

AN OPEN DOOR

Put your heart and mind into teaching and helping students learn. You may lack some desired competence at first, but there is always the probability of gaining effectiveness with experience according to your personal aspirations and abilities. Support from other professionals and friends can be helpful. Above all, there must be the blessings of God from whom all blessings flow. If a person strongly desires to teach, this is an area into which there is always an open door. It can be found by checking and seeking for opportunities. Remember that open doors require preparedness and/or willingness to become prepared. Pursue and continue to pursue, but with the kingdom of God and His righteousness foremost in your seeking.

APT TO TEACH

"Can the blind lead the blind? Shall they not both fall into the ditch?" (Luke 6:39). In-depth theological and scriptural training are of great value for the Christian teacher. Nevertheless, the teacher needs ability and communication skills to guide students to have valuable and meaningful learning experiences. Resources can enhance the teaching activity. I have concluded that Luther's Small Catechism is second only to the Bible as an incomparable resource for teaching children and adults the important fundamentals of the Christian religion. Also, Luther's question-and-answer technique of the 16th century is still a timely and effective approach for teaching God's basic truths as we enter the 21st century. Dialog between teacher and students triggering interaction among students and instructor is wholesome and escalating for the teaching-learning process. This alludes to the worth of teachers taking one or more courses in human development for better understanding of students' nature, traits, and characteristics as human beings.

SITUATIONAL TEACHING

Generally, formal educational activities in a church or school are ideal for full-time church workers. There are usually audiovisuals and other educational materials. However, teaching persons through learning experiences can occur in everyday situations informally. Following Jesus' model, we can use earthly things to teach spiritual meaning, as using the farmer to sow the Word of God like seed. The Christian-education teacher can employ life situations, e.g., sickness, employment, loss or gain of property, and other things as lessons in "casting all your care upon Him; for He careth for you" (1 Peter 5:7). The foregoing thinking about teaching demonstrates a vibrant and visible overlap of teaching and effective strategies utilized by some pastors during preaching.

Finally, I am sharing thoughtworthy statements from two of my mentors and friends. Thirty years ago, the late Dr. Paul Bergevin of the graduate school at Indiana University advised the following:

- Avoid extremes
- Love wisdom
- Seek knowledge
- Search for truth
- Pursue excellence.

Moreover, the prayerful words quoted by Dr. Albert Dominick at my seminary graduation direct us to the source and purpose for wisdom and knowledge. "Now, O LORD God, ... Give me now wisdom and knowledge, that I may go out and come in before this people" (2 Chronicles 1:9–10).

Henry C. King Sr.
(Papa)

The newlyweds,
Robert H. and Jean King,
in 1949.

The 16 children and stepmother
on the day of Papa's funeral.

The theological students of Immanuel Lutheran College.
From left to right:
O. R. Thompson, Howard A. Foard, Robert H. King,
George R. Wyatt, and William H. Griffen. One student,
Wilbur Morgan, was absent when the picture was taken.

Dr. Rosa J. Young, teacher at Rosebud and matron at Alabama Lutheran Academy, Selma.

Chineta Lawhorn Riley, teacher and missionary in Alabama schools. Matron at Alabama Lutheran Academy, Selma.

Rev. Marmaduke N. Carter, served with Rosa Young in Alabama mission work. Lectured in the Midwest to promote mission support for Alabama. Founder of St. Philip Congregation, Chicago, Ill.

Rev. Peter R. Hunt, served several Alabama rural congregations. Dean of Students, professor, and president pro tem, Concordia College, Selma.

The Robert H. King family. From left to right: Jann, Roger, Jocelyn, Jean, and Robert.

Dr. King with grandson, Casey.

Dr. King with Concordia University Austin President David
Zersen. Dr. King was commencement speaker.